Stewed to the Gills

STEWED TO THE GILLS

FISH AND WINE COOKERY

BY
ESTHER LEWIN & BIRDINA LEWIN

ILLUSTRATED BY
JAY RIVKIN

NASH PUBLISHING, LOS ANGELES

Copyright © 1971 by Esther Lewin and Birdina Lewin

All rights reserved. No part of this book may be reproduced in any form or by any means without permission in writing from the publisher.

Library of Congress Catalog Card Number: 70-160164
Standard Book Number: 8402-1203-8

Published simultaneously in the United States and Canada by Nash Publishing, 9255 Sunset Boulevard, Los Angeles, California 90069.

Printed in the United States of America

First printing

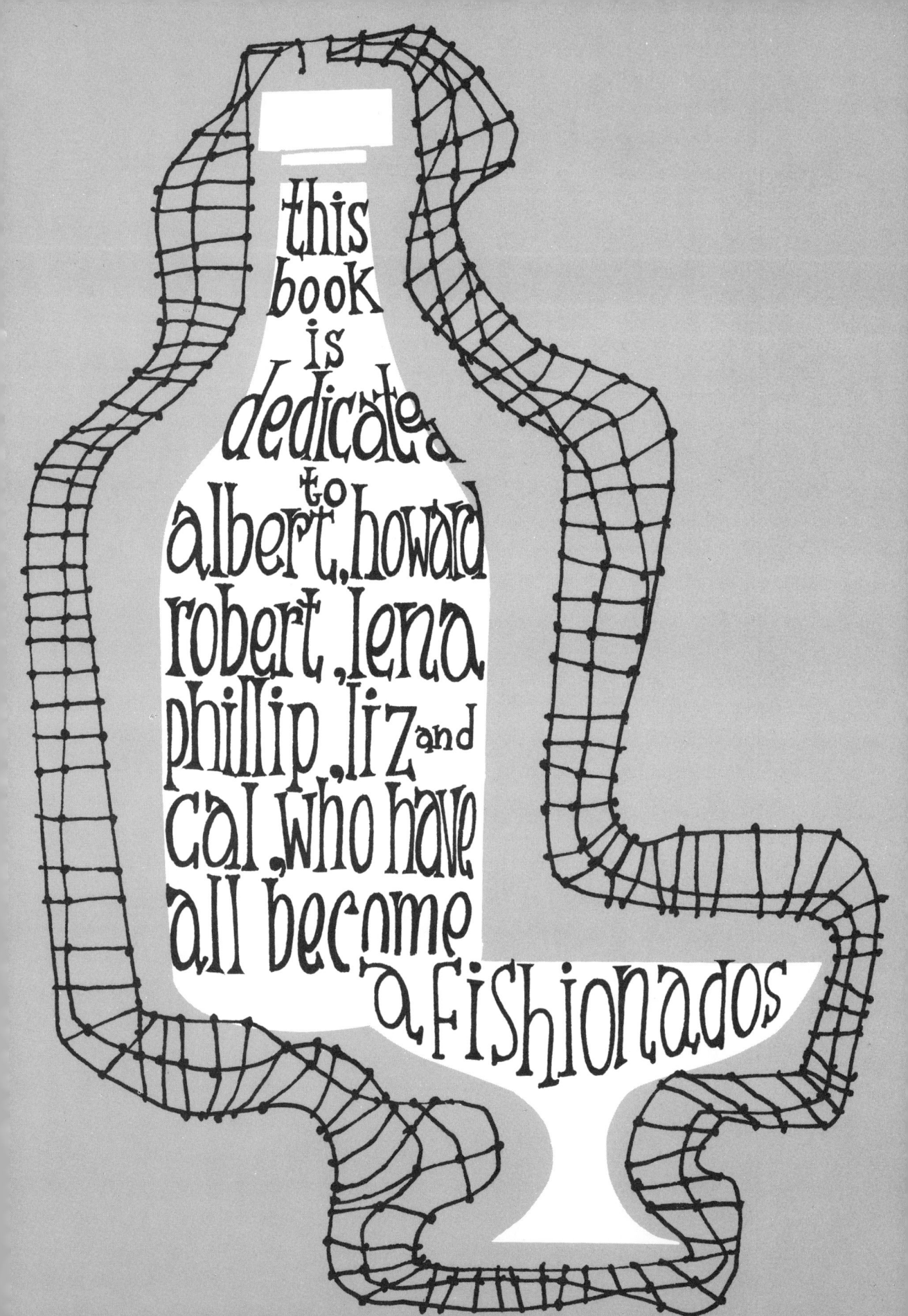

DOWN TO THE SEA IN SCHNAPPS 13
Halibut • Bass • Salmon

NAME YOUR POISSON 43
Sole • Flounder • Sand Dabs

OFF THE DEEP END 61
Red Snapper • Cod • Pike • Barracuda • Trout

STEWED TO THE GILLS 75
A Fine Kettle of Assorted Fish

TUNA TIES ONE ON 95

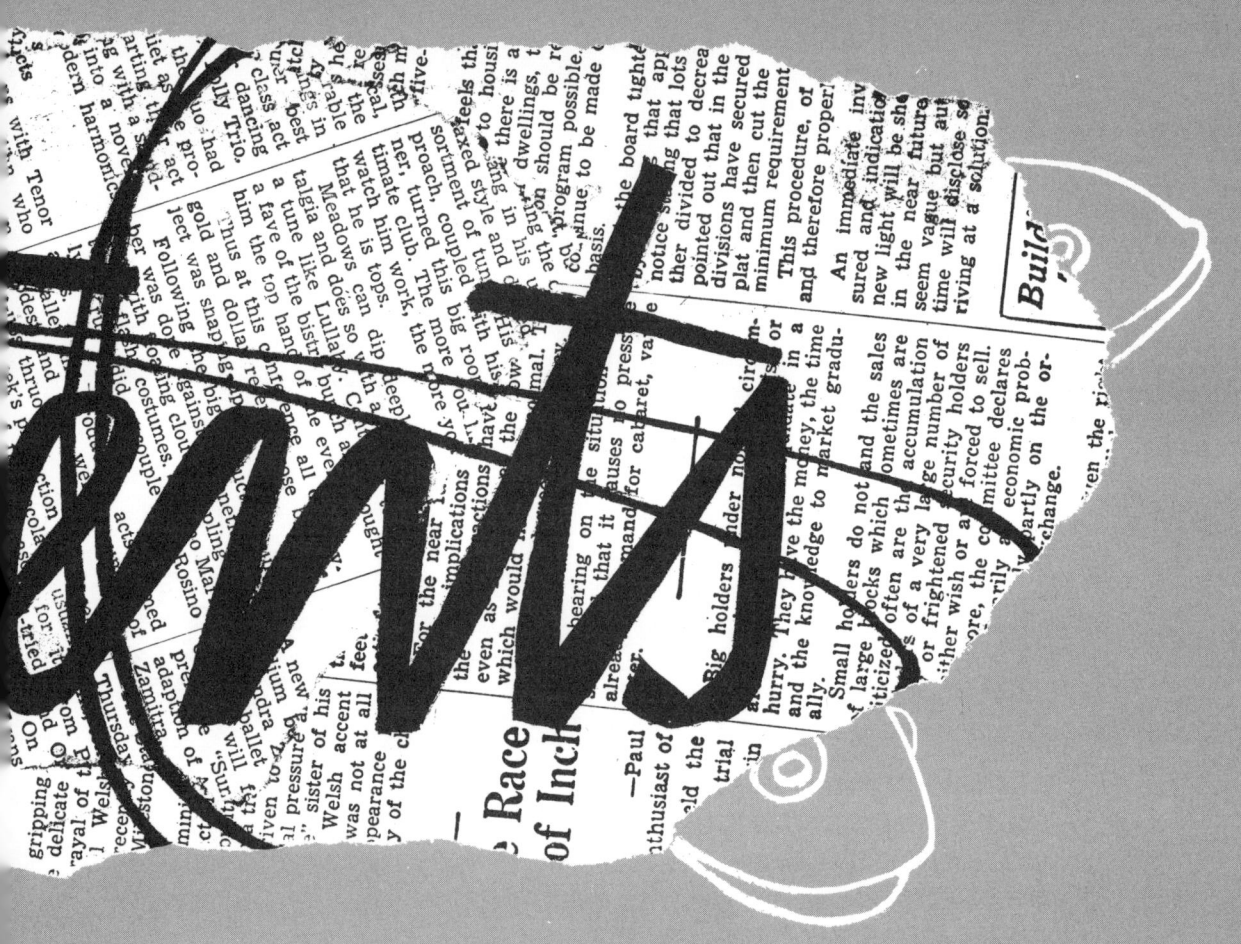

SOUSED, SAUCED, SMASHED,
SHICKERED, SPIKED, SOAKED AND SWIZZLED   103
Shrimp

CROCKED CRAB   125

ALL TANKED UP   141
Lobster • Clams • Oysters • Mussels • Scallops

ON THE WAGON   161

Stewed to the Gills

No one has ever written a cookbook that got banned in Boston—or sold to the movies for that "scene" in the kitchen. However a fact has occurred to us that could arouse a tsk or two about fish. No, none of that stuff about upstream, downstream or what goes on with mermaids.

The truth is that fish have taken to alcohol. We're not accusing them of being secret drinkers, for it's well known that all fish are strictly water oriented. But a fish out of water does better if it heads straight for the bar.

For fish have a natural affinity for wine. What fish wouldn't rather swim in champagne—or be bathed in chablis? But since nature didn't arrange it that way and no good-hearted vintner has offered to dump his total production into the sea to satisfy this urge, we've provided a happy substitute. Here is a collection of fish recipes all enhanced by the addition of wine, mellow and aromatic, from sun-drenched vineyards. Sometimes adding wine makes a subtle sea-change, sometimes a bold strike. For those of you who think a fish is just a fish, we suggest you try "Brandy Snappers" or "Fish Cantina" or any other of the following recipes. You'll agree the poor fish has indeed become sublime.

CHAPTER ONE

DOWN TO THE SEA IN SCHNAPPS

Fish Cantina

2 lbs. halibut, sea bass or cod, cut in lengths 1 inch wide
1 teaspoon olive oil
2 tomatoes, sliced thin
1 green pepper or pimiento chopped coarsely
2 large onions, sliced thin
2 dozen Greek olives
2 cloves garlic, finely chopped
½ teaspoon saffron threads
1 cup dry white wine
2 large potatoes, sliced thin
¼ cup olive oil
1¼ teaspoon salt
¼ teaspoon pepper

Rub a teaspoon of olive oil around the sides and bottom of a large casserole. Put the tomatoes on the bottom of the casserole. Salt lightly, add the pepper or pimiento over the tomatoes and salt lightly. Lay the onion slices over the pepper and salt lightly. Lay fish on top of onions and salt lightly. Place the Greek olives and garlic over the fish. Add saffron to wine and pour over fish. Arrange layers of potatoes over fish. Sprinkle with black pepper and remaining salt. Drizzle ¼ cup olive oil over potatoes. Bake uncovered in a 300° oven until potatoes are golden and tender (about 1 hour). Serve with French bread. Serves 6.

Rake's Halibut

4 slices halibut, ¾ inch thick
1 large can prune plums, drained, peeled and pitted
½ cup ketchup
2 tablespoons dark brown sugar
1 tablespoon lemon juice
½ cup dry sherry
3 tablespoons butter or margarine, melted
½ teaspoon salt
¼ teaspoon pepper

Combine plums, ketchup, lemon juice and brown sugar in blender for 1 minute. Marinate the halibut in this sauce for 4 hours, turning the fish at least once to coat all the sides. Drain fish well. In a small saucepan combine the marinade, sherry and butter, and heat. Place the fish on the barbecue or under the broiler, brush with some sauce and broil 8 minutes on each side—no longer! Salt and pepper the fish and pass the hot sauce. Serves 4.

Halibut Burgundy

3 lbs. halibut, sliced
1 medium onion, diced
1 small green pepper, diced
2 cloves garlic, minced
2 tablespoons butter or margarine
3 tablespoons oil
2 tablespoons Burgundy
1 lemon or lime
1 teaspoon dried or fresh parsley
1 large tomato, diced
½ teaspoon salt
¼ teaspoon pepper

Sauté the onion, garlic and green pepper in butter and 2 tablespoons oil, until golden. Add tomato and parsley and continue to sauté until onions are brown. Salt and pepper the fish and place in a shallow pan. Drizzle remaining oil, lemon or lime juice and wine over fish. Bake in a 350° oven for 20 minutes or until fish is done. Remove to serving dish and spread heated sauce over each piece of fish. Serves 6.

Halibut, Bouquet du Vin

2 lbs. fillet of halibut
4 tablespoons butter or margarine
1 medium onion, sliced
¼ cup wine vinegar
¼ cup dry red wine
1 tablespoon sugar
1 tablespoon currants
1 tablespoon pine nuts
½ pint sour cream
1 teaspoon salt
½ teaspoon pepper

Season the halibut with half of the salt and pepper. Place fish in a shallow oven-to-table casserole, dot with half of the butter. Bake in a 400° oven for 10 minutes or until fish is done. While fish is cooking, sauté onion in rest of butter until golden. Add vinegar, wine, sugar, currants, pine nuts, sour cream and rest of salt and pepper. Cook until hot. Pour over fish and return to oven for 2 or 3 minutes. Serves 6.

Halibut Kanpai!

4 halibut steaks
¼ teaspoon salt
juice of half a lemon
¼ cup saki
½ cup soy sauce
2 tablespoons butter or margarine
½ teaspoon freshly grated ginger

Sprinkle halibut with salt, juice of the lemon and saki. Place fish in a pan that can go under broiler. Pour soy sauce over fish and let stand for at least 30 minutes. Dot the fish with butter and sprinkle ginger over each piece. Broil for about 12 minutes or until done. Baste several times. Serves 4.

Bartenders' Halibut

4 slices halibut or other firm fish
2 tablespoons capers and juice
4 tablespoons butter or margarine
2 tablespoons dry vermouth
1 lemon
½ teaspoon salt
¼ teaspoon pepper

Sauté the halibut in butter until brown on both sides. When fish is almost done, sprinkle with salt and pepper, the juice from half of the lemon, and vermouth. Spoon the capers and a little of the caper juice over the fish. Slice the other half of the lemon thin and lay the slices over the fish. Cover for a few minutes and then serve. Serves 4.

Halibut Santé

4 serving-size halibut steaks
2 tablespoons dry sherry
½ teaspoon salt
½ pint sour cream at room temperature
2 large cloves garlic
¼ cup grated Parmesan cheese

Put the steaks in a greased baking dish. Drizzle sherry over fish. Sprinkle salt over fish. Give the sour cream a dozen brisk whisks with a spoon to make it light and fluffy. Put the garlic through a garlic press and mix with sour cream. Spoon the cream over halibut until it is about ½ inch thick. Top lightly with cheese and bake in a 375° oven for 30 minutes. Serves 4.

Oiled Halibut

4 halibut steaks
3 tablespoons butter or margarine
1 small can anchovies
juice of 1 lemon
2 tablespoons dry vermouth

Put halibut in a greased shallow pan. Dot with butter and broil 10 minutes or until done. While steaks are broiling, put the anchovies, including oil, in a small pan on a low flame. Add wine and the juice of the lemon and mix. Put the steaks on a serving platter and pour the sauce over them. Serves 4.

Guzzler's Fish

6 slices halibut
1/3 cup dry sherry
1/3 cup lime juice
1/4 cup melted butter or margarine
1/2 teaspoon salt
1/4 teaspoon freshly ground pepper
generous pinch marjoram
1 can frozen cream of shrimp soup, thawed
1/2 cup sour cream at room temperature
4 green onions, sliced thin
1/2 cup tiny cooked shrimp

Place halibut in a shallow baking dish. Pour the sherry and lime juice over the fish and marinate for 5 minutes on each side. Discard the juice. Pour butter over the fish and sprinkle with the seasoning and marjoram. Broil for 10 minutes. Remove from heat and baste with pan juices. Set aside to cool slightly. Mix soup and sour cream together and spoon over the halibut. Bake for 15 minutes in a 325° oven. Sprinkle tiny shrimp and green onions over fish and serve immediately. Serves 6.

Poisson, Carafe

2 lbs. thinly sliced halibut, bass, sole or other firm fish	1 teaspoon mace
	½ teaspoon salt
2 tablespoons butter or margarine	1 teaspoon grated lemon rind
	2 teaspoons arrowroot
2 teaspoons onion powder	3 tablespoons lemon juice
1 teaspoon Mei Yen powder	1 egg
¼ teaspoon ground or powdered ginger	½ cup dry white wine
	½ cup water
½ teaspoon white pepper	½ teaspoon saffron threads

In a large heavy skillet, sauté the onion powder very slowly in the butter for at least 5 minutes. Wipe the pieces of fish very dry, and brown on both sides in the skillet. Turn heat low, cover skillet, and simmer 10 minutes. Place all the other ingredients except water, wine and saffron in a bowl and blend well. Dissolve saffron in water, add wine and combine with the egg and seasoning mixture. Pour on and around fish while lifting the pieces gently with a wide spatula. Turn heat up until sauce is bubbling, then reduce heat. Cover skillet and cook for an additional minute. The sauce will become smooth and creamy without stirring. Serves 6.

Halibut With Rice Wine

4 thick slices halibut	½ teaspoon freshly grated ginger
1 onion, chopped	
1 cup clam juice	½ lb. bacon
½ cup brown sugar	¼ teaspoon coarse kosher salt
½ cup rice wine	

Marinate the fish in all the ingredients (except bacon and salt) for at least 4 hours. Remove fish from marinade and place in a large, shallow oven-to-table dish. Strain the marinade over the fish and bake in a 350° oven for 30 minutes. While fish is baking, fry or broil bacon very crisp. When fish is done, remove from oven, sprinkle with coarse salt and lay strips of bacon across the top. Serves 4.

Halibut, Bottoms Up!

6 halibut steaks
juice of one lemon
1¼ cups dry white wine
1 egg
½ teaspoon salt
⅛ teaspoon pepper

4 tablespoons butter or margarine
1 tablespoon green onions, chopped fine
1 tablespoon chopped parsley

Put halibut in a shallow dish. Mix the juice of half the lemon, 1 cup wine, salt, pepper and egg. Pour over the fish and marinate for an hour. Lift fish from marinade and save marinade. Heat 2 tablespoons butter in a large skillet. Sauté fish on both sides until done and golden. While fish is sautéing, melt the remaining butter in a saucepan. Add ¼ cup of the marinade, remaining lemon juice and ¼ cup wine. Bring to a boil. Put fish on serving platter. Pour sauce over fish. Sprinkle with chopped green onions and parsley. Serves 6.

Down to the Sea in Schnapps

Whiskey Sour Fish

3 lbs. halibut, bass, sole or
   other firm fish
1 6-oz. can concentrated
   frozen lemonade
2 tablespoons bourbon
1 8-oz. can tomato sauce
¼ teaspoon salt
¼ teaspoon pepper
¼ teaspoon seasoned salt
1 medium onion, sliced
½ green pepper, sliced

Defrost frozen lemonade and mix with tomato sauce and bourbon. Put the onion and green pepper slices on the bottom of a casserole. Lay the fish on the onions and peppers. Season with salt, pepper and seasoned salt. Pour sauce over the fish and bake in a 400° oven for 20 minutes or until fish is done. Baste frequently. Serves 6.

Cakes and Ale

3 lbs. halibut, in one piece
½ onion, grated
1 egg
½ teaspoon salt
1 teaspoon soy sauce
1 teaspoon ale, beer or
   dry sherry
1 scant tablespoon
   cornstarch
½ cup milk
oil for frying

Peel skin from fish and with a fork scrape the fish from the bones until you have about 2 cups raw fish. Or, grind fish twice in meat grinder. Combine all the ingredients. If the mixture is too thin to form into small flat cakes, add a little more cornstarch. Fry quickly in hot oil until crisp and brown. Can be eaten hot or cold. Serves 4.

Poisson au Bistro

1½ lbs. fillet of halibut, haddock or cod
1 teaspoon salt
½ teaspoon garlic salt
½ teaspoon MSG or Accent
¼ teaspoon thyme
¼ teaspoon oregano
⅛ teaspoon fennel
¼ teaspoon pepper
1 small bay leaf, crushed
1 onion, sliced thin
⅔ cup half and half
⅓ cup dry sherry

Put fish in a lightly greased, shallow baking dish and sprinkle with seasonings and bay leaf. Cover fish with sliced onion and pour cream and sherry over all. Bake uncovered in a 350° oven for 25 minutes. Serves 4–5.

Connoisseur's Halibut

1½ cups cold, cooked flaked halibut
2 egg yolks
1½ tablespoons butter or margarine
½ tablespoon instant or granular flour
2 teaspoons sugar
¼ teaspoon Tabasco
1 teaspoon dry mustard
¼ cup vinegar
¾ cup cream
½ teaspoon salt
¼ teaspoon white pepper
dash of paprika
1 envelope unflavored gelatin
2 tablespoons clam juice
watercress

Combine all the ingredients, except halibut, clam juice, gelatin and watercress. Cook them in a double boiler until thick. Remove

Down to the Sea in Schnapps

from fire. Dissolve the gelatin in the clam juice and add to the warm mixture. Stir in the halibut. Pour into an oiled 4-cup mold. Chill until very firm. Unmold on watercress and serve with white wine sauce. Serves 6.

White Wine Sauce

1 cup stiffly beaten whipped cream
2 egg whites, beaten stiffly with ½ teaspoon salt
1 tablespoon chablis
1 cucumber, chopped, well drained

Fold together all ingredients immediately before serving.

Bass With a Head On

4 slices bass or red snapper
¼ lb. tiny cooked shrimp
1 tablespoon mayonnaise
1 teaspoon dry vermouth
pinch MSG or Accent
½ teaspoon salt
1 egg white, stiffly beaten
¼ teaspoon pepper
1 egg white, stiffly beaten
2 tablespoons butter or margarine

Salt and pepper fish. Dot lightly with butter and place in a greased, shallow pan. Broil until the fish is done (about 10 minutes). While fish is broiling, mix shrimp, mayonnaise, vermouth and MSG. Fold into stiffly beaten egg white. When fish is done, pile shrimp mixture on it. Broil for 2 minutes until puffed and lightly browned. Serves 4.

Bass Bacchanal

4 serving slices bass
8 medium shrimp, cooked and shelled
4 heaping tablespoons chutney
3 tablespoons sweet vermouth
4 heaping tablespoons bread crumbs
4 tablespoons butter or margarine
4 pieces bacon, cooked and crumbled
2 tablespoons oil

Put oil in bottom of shallow casserole that goes from oven to table. Lay bass in casserole and broil until almost done. Thin chutney with vermouth. Melt butter and mix with bread crumbs. Arrange 2 shrimp on each piece of bass. Spread chutney over bass and shrimp. Sprinkle bacon over chutney. Sprinkle bread crumbs over all. Return to broiler for 1–2 minutes. Serve with rice. Serves 4.

Tippler's Bass

2 lbs. bass or corbina fillets
1 cup milk
1 teaspoon salt
¾ cup bread crumbs
½ teaspoon seasoned salt
¼ teaspoon pepper
3 tablespoons butter

Dip fish in milk to which salt has been added. Roll fish in bread crumbs and lay in a greased shallow baking dish. Sprinkle with seasoned salt and pepper, dot with butter and bake in a 400° oven for 15 minutes or until fish is done. Serve with mustard sauce. Serves 6.

Mustard Sauce

1 cup mayonnaise
½ teaspoon dry mustard
1 tablespoon grated onion

1 tablespoon dry sherry
juice of ½ lemon
dash salt

Combine all ingredients thoroughly.

Taproom Bass

6 slices bass, quartered
2 onions, sliced
6 potatoes
1½ teaspoons salt
½ teaspoon pepper

2 tablespoons butter or margarine
¼ cup dry white wine
water

Sauté onions in butter in deep skillet or Dutch oven until onions are very brown. Put fish on the onions. Season the fish, using half of the salt and pepper. Peel and slice the potatoes 2 inches thick. Put the sliced potatoes over the fish and season with the remaining salt and pepper. Add enough water to cover all. Add wine. Cover and cook on a low flame for about an hour or until the potatoes are done. Serve in soup bowls, because this dish tastes like fish and potatoes in French onion soup and you won't want to miss any of the broth. It's heavenly! Serves 6.

Bass Trattoria

2 lbs. bass
¼ cup minced onion
3 tablespoons olive oil
3 cups cooked or canned
    tomatoes, drained
2 whole cloves
1 teaspoon salt
¼ teaspoon pepper
3 tablespoons flour
¼ cup chianti
½ cup stuffed green olives
½ cup celery, chopped
2 tablespoons capers, drained
3 tablespoons parlsey,
    chopped

Cook the onion in oil until very soft. Add the tomatoes, cloves, salt and pepper. Cover and simmer for 15 minutes. Make a paste of the flour and wine. Stir into tomatoes and cook for 5 minutes. Add olives, celery, capers and parsley. Put the fish in a greased baking pan. Pour the sauce over the fish. Bake in a 375° oven 30 minutes. Baste often. Serves 4–5.

Eye-Opener Bass

2 lbs. bass or cod, cut in
    serving pieces
1 package frozen lima beans
8–10 carrots
6 medium potatoes
½ cup dry white wine
⅛ teaspoon allspice
1 medium onion, cut in half
1 bay leaf crumbled
1 teaspoon salt
¼ teaspoon freshly ground
    pepper
water to cover fish

Cook lima beans, carrots and potatoes in separate pans. As the vegetables are cooking, poach the fish and onions in the remaining ingredients. Serve fish and vegetables on a large platter. Everyone fills his plate with fish and vegetables and then spoons garlic sauce over all. Serves 6.

Eye-Opener Garlic Sauce

6 cloves garlic
juice of 1 lemon

2 cups mayonnaise

Press garlic through a press or pulverize with a mortar and pestle. Add to mayonnaise and lemon juice and mix thoroughly.

Boozy Bass

6 slices bass
2 tablespoons oil
1 teaspoon salt
1/4 teaspoon pepper
1 large onion, chopped fine
2 green onions, thinly sliced
1 large clove garlic, minced

2 medium tomatoes, peeled and chopped
1/2 teaspoon sweet basil
1/2 teaspoon thyme
1 cup dry white wine
juice of 1 lemon
3 tablespoons chopped parsley

Salt and pepper fish and place in an oil-rubbed baking pan. Mix onions, garlic and tomatoes together and spread over fish. Add wine, sweet basil and thyme. Place in a 400° oven for 30 minutes. Put fish on a serving platter and cool. Transfer sauce to a saucepan and cook over medium heat until it is almost completely reduced. Correct seasoning with salt and pepper. Cool sauce. When sauce and fish are both cold, spoon sauce over fish. Drizzle lemon juice over sauce and sprinkle with chopped parsley. Serves 6.

Cocoloco Bass

2 lbs. sea bass
1 can undiluted cream of celery soup
1 teaspoon chopped onion
2 tablespoons shredded coconut
⅓ cup milk
¼ cup dry white wine
pinch sweet basil
2 tablespoons slivered almonds

Arrange fish in a greased casserole. Mix celery soup, onion, coconut, milk, wine and sweet basil. Pour over fish, Sprinkle with slivered almonds. Cover with foil and bake in a 350° oven for 30 minutes. Serves 4–5.

Tutava Tequila

4 pieces tutava or bass fillets
½ pint sour cream
1 small can chili salsa
1 tablespoon tequila or dry white wine
cayenne

Put fish in greased casserole. Mix sour cream, chili salsa and tequila. Pour over fish and bake in a 400° oven for 12 minutes or until fish is done. Sprinkle lightly with cayenne. Serves 4.

Down to the Sea in Schnapps

Saki-Eyed Salmon

4 salmon steaks
2 tablespoons butter or margarine
½ teaspoon salt
¼ teaspoon pepper
8 tablespoons butter or margarine
1 clove garlic, crushed
2 tablespoons soy sauce
1 teaspoon saki
1 tablespoon prepared mustard
2 tablespoons ketchup
½ teaspoon Worcestershire sauce

Put the salmon in a broiling pan. Season with salt and pepper. Dot with 2 tablespoons butter. Broil 12 minutes until done. Combine all other ingredients in a double boiler over hot water. Beat with an egg beater until hot. Pour over salmon and serve immediately.

Winemaker's Salmon

4 salmon steaks
1 small cucumber, unpeeled
2 tablespoons chablis
juice of ½ lemon
½ teaspoon salt
¼ teaspoon pepper
1 onion, sliced thin
2 tomatoes, sliced
1 teaspoon dill weed
½ pint sour cream

Place salmon steaks in a well-greased dish or pan. Sprinkle wine and lemon juice over fish and salt and pepper the steaks. Grate the cucumber, drain thoroughly and spoon over fish. Lay onion slices over the cucumber and top the onions with the tomato slices. Sprinkle the dill over the tomatoes. Cover all with sour cream. Bake in a 350° oven for 25 minutes. Spoon off any excess liquid while cooking. Serves 4.

Nip of Salmon

4 salmon steaks
½ cup mayonnaise
1 tablespoon lemon juice
1 tablespoon dry white wine
½ teaspoon salt
¼ teaspoon pepper

Season the salmon with salt and pepper. Thin the mayonnaise with the lemon juice and wine and mix thoroughly. Coat both sides of the salmon with the mayonnaise and broil in a shallow pan for 10 minutes until brown and bubbly. Serves 4.

Salmon in High Spirits

4 salmon steaks
4 tablespoons butter or margarine
½ teaspoon salt
1 cup dry white wine

Place salmon steaks in a shallow pan. Pour the wine over the fish. Salt steaks and put a tablespoon of butter on each. Broil for 10 minutes or until salmon is done. Baste often. Remove salmon to serving platter and pour pan juices over fish. Serves 4.

Vintage California Salmon

6 salmon steaks
8 tablespoons butter or margarine
3 tablespoons sauterne
juice of 1 large lemon
1 teaspoon dried parsley
¼ teaspoon coarse black pepper
½ teaspoon salt

One of the best ways to serve salmon is barbecued on an open fire, well basted with butter and lemon. If you can't manage an open fire, broil it in lemon sauce. Melt the butter, add the wine, lemon juice and parsley and simmer for a few minutes. Salt and pepper the salmon steaks and place on greased broiler tray. Spoon half of the butter sauce over fish. Broil for 12 minutes, basting with pan juices and rest of butter sauce. Put the fish on a serving platter. Scrape the bottom of the pan and pour the butter sauce over fish. Serves 6.

Pickled Fish

6 thin slices of fillet of salmon about 2 inches wide and 5 inches long
6 thin slices of fillet of sole, about the same size
6 long flat slices of dill pickle, about ⅛ inch thick
¼ teaspoon dill weed
1 cup dry white wine

Put slices of the dill pickle between slices of salmon and sole, and roll. Secure the rolls with a piece of string or skewer. Put the rolls in a greased baking pan. Sprinkle with dill weed. Add wine so that fish is half covered. Cover the pan and bake in a 400° oven for 20 minutes. Serves 3.

Salmon in Its Cups

1 3–4 lb. piece of salmon
1½ cups prepared stuffing mix
2 tablespoons chopped onions
4 tablespoons butter or margarine
2 tablespoons chopped parsley
2 tablespoons chopped celery tops
1 egg, beaten
½ teaspoon dry tarragon, crushed
2 tablespoons capers
2 tablespoons dry vermouth
juice of 1 lemon
½ teaspoon seasoned salt
¼ teaspoon pepper

Brown onions in butter. Combine stuffing mix, celery tops, chopped parsley, egg, tarragon, capers and onions. Lay fish on aluminum foil in a baking dish. Stuff fish and secure stuffiing with skewers. Sprinkle vermouth and lemon juice over fish and season with the seasoned salt and pepper. Wrap in foil and bake in a 375° oven for about ¾ hour. Unwrap the fish for the last 5 minutes so that it will brown. Serves 6.

Salmon Cabaret

1 4–5 lb. whole or piece of salmon	2 tablespoons capers
1 small onion, chopped	½ teaspoon dill weed
2 tablespoons butter or margarine	4 tablespoons butter or margarine, melted
1½ cups soft, fresh white bread crumbs	1 teaspoon salt
3 tablespoons chopped celery	2 tablespoons dry sherry
dash of cayenne	juice of ½ lemon
	1 large onion, sliced thin

Brown chopped onions in 2 tablespoons butter and set aside. Line a baking pan with sufficient aluminum foil to wrap the fish. Lay the fish on the foil. Combine bread crumbs (make them in the blender), fried onions, celery, cayenne, capers, dill weed, butter and salt. If necessary, add more butter to make stuffing hold together. Stuff fish. Secure stuffing with skewers. Sprinkle fish with wine and lemon juice and cover top with thinly sliced onions. Cover fish with foil and bake in a 350° oven for 1 hour. Serves 8.

Salmon From the Winery

1 3–4 lb. piece of salmon	½ cup dry sherry
1 8-oz. bottle green goddess salad dressing	

Place fish in a greased shallow baking pan, preferably one that can also be used for serving. Mix dressing and sherry and pour over fish. Bake in a 350° oven for 1 hour. Serves 6.

Sommelier's Poached Salmon Français

The court bouillon in which this salmon is cooked can be used as a fish broth or stock for such dishes as bouillabaise, cioppino or fish chowder. There are many variations to poaching fish and for the court bouillon. The one below is a classic recipe. Change it as you will or do it just as it is.

1 7-lb. piece of salmon   or   6 - 7 lbs. of salmon cut into 1½-inch slices

Court Bouillon

2 quarts water	1 bay leaf
1 cup sauterne	½ teaspoon dry thyme
½ cup wine vinegar	5 sprigs parsley
2 carrots, sliced	1 tablespoon salt
2 onions, sliced	10 whole black peppercorns

[handwritten annotation: Celery]

Combine all the court bouillon ingredients in a large fish kettle, a skillet or other large pot. Tie the fish in a cheesecloth. It's much easier to remove when done. Lower fish into the court bouillon. Simmer on the lowest possible flame so that the broth is barely moving. Cook about 8 minutes to a pound after it has started to simmer. If you are cooking pieces of fish, simmer the court bouillon for about 45 minutes before adding fish. Cook pieces of fish for 35–40 minutes. Fish to be served cold should be cooled in the court bouillon. Salmon served hot is lifted from the broth immediately by lifting the ends of the cheesecloth. Unwrap it on a serving platter and garnish with parsley and lemon wedges, and sprinkle with paprika. Many sauces can be served with poached salmon. Serves 10.

Stoned Cold Salmon With Sauce Verte

1 7-lb. piece of salmon, poached according to directions for SOMMELIER'S POACHED SALMON (see p. 33) and cooled

Sauce Verte

2 pints sour cream
2 cucumbers, peeled and chopped fine
3 green onions, chopped fine
2 cups mayonnaise
few drops green vegetable coloring (optional)
½ teaspoon dry mustard, a little at a time according to taste

Combine all ingredients and mix well.

Arrange salmon on a platter and garnish with parsley. Additional garnishes may be artichoke hearts, sliced hard-boiled eggs and chilled braised celery (made by cooking for 20 minutes 4-inch lengths of celery in water and bouillon cubes, salt and pepper, drained well and chilled. Serve sauce separately. Serves 10.

Sweet Adeline's Cold Salmon Chaud Froid

1 7-lb. piece of salmon, poached and cooled as in SOMMELIER'S POACHED SALMON (see p. 33)
1½ cups COURT BOUILLON (see p. 33)
1 envelope unflavored gelatin
½ cup mayonnaise

Soften gelatin in ½ cup court bouillon. Heat remaining court bouillon. Add softened gelatin mixture to hot bouillon and mix well. Allow to cool. Add mayonnaise and mix well. Chill until slightly thickened. Spread over cold salmon. Refrigerate until ready to serve, allowing enough time for gelatin to set. You may decorate salmon with capers and sliced green olives to form the head and tail of a fish. Garnish with flowered radishes, beets, onions and cucumbers. Serves 10.

Salmon Out Cold

1 7-lb. piece of salmon	1 teaspoon salt
juice of 1 lemon	½ teaspoon pepper
½ cup dry white wine	2 medium onions, sliced

Put the salmon on a piece of aluminum foil large enough to wrap the fish securely. Sprinkle salmon with lemon juice, wine, salt and pepper. Spread onions over fish and wrap it well. Place in a shallow baking pan and bake in a 325° oven for 1½ hours. Cool before serving.

OR

Put the fish in a baking dish. Drizzle wine and lemon over fish. Dot with 4 tablespoons butter or margarine. Sprinkle with salt and pepper and cover with onions. Cover and bake in a 325° oven for 1½ hours or until fish is done. Cool fish and serve with a sauce or lemon. Serves 10.

Salmon Alaska, Grand Crus

2 cups flaked canned salmon, boned
2 envelopes unflavored gelatin
¼ cup water
¼ cup boiling clam juice
½ cup mayonnaise
2 tablespoons chopped green onions
1 tablespoon lemon juice
1 tablespoon dry vermouth
1½ teaspoons salt
½ teaspoon white pepper
½ cup heavy whipped cream
6 egg whites (large size eggs)
⅛ teaspoon cream of tartar
¼ teaspoon onion salt

Soak gelatin in the cold water and then dissolve it in the boiling clam juice. Add the lemon juice and vermouth. Cool. Stir in mayonnaise, green onions, salt and pepper. Whip the cream very stiff, fold it into the mixture and chill until almost set. Fold in the fish. Place in a small oiled loaf pan. The pan should hold about 3 cups and the mixture should almost fill the pan. Chill until very firm. Unmold onto a bread board that has been covered with heavy paper or parchment and cover fish with a very stiff meringue made by beating egg whites, cream of tartar and onion salt. Bake in a 375° oven just until brown. Watch it carefully. This should take no more than 4 or 5 minutes. Use the paper to slide the loaf to a serving dish. Serve immediately. Serves 6.

Salmon Cooler

6 salmon steaks, cut 1 inch thick
½ teaspoon salt
2 tablespoons pickling spices
3 cups water
¼ cup dry white wine
1½ cups vinegar
½ cup sugar
¼ cup white raisins
2 medium onions, chopped
1 3-oz. package of lemon-flavored gelatin

Salt the fish and refrigerate for an hour. Put the water in a large pot. Add the vinegar, wine, sugar, raisins, and onions. Put the pickling spices in a spice bag or make one by tying the spices in a square of cheesecloth or any cotton fabric. Drop the spice bag into the water and boil for about 15 minutes. Wash salt from fish and put it in the boiling water so that the pieces do not overlap. Taste the water. It should have a vinegary taste. Boil gently for 20 minutes. Dissolve the gelatin in cup of hot fish broth. Then add to pot. Boil for another minute. Turn off the fire and let the fish sit in the broth until lukewarm. Lift the fish very carefully out of the pot onto a deep heat-proof dish. Let the fish cool for about 15 minutes and then pour the broth over the fish. Decorate with some of the spices from the spice bag. Garnish with slices of lemon around the edge of the dish. Cool for another 15 minutes and refrigerate to set the gelatin. Garnish with fresh parsley. Serves 6.

Potted Salmon

1 lb. smoked salmon
1 teaspoon dry vermouth
1 teaspoon lemon juice
1–2 tablespoons fine fresh
   bread crumbs

12 tiny cream puff shells or
   small rounds of toast
capers

Cut salmon into small pieces with kitchen shears. Put a few pieces at a time into blender with a drop or two of the lemon juice and vermouth. Repeat this procedure until all of the salmon is smooth. Scrape all the contents into a bowl. If the mixture is too liquid, add bread crumbs gradually until a stiffer consistency is reached. Fill cream puff shells or pile lightly on toast rounds and decorate with capers. Serve as a first course or appetizer. Serves 4.

Plastered Salmon

1 1-lb. can pink salmon, boned and flaked	1 onion, grated
½ can cream of mushroom soup	1 hard-boiled egg, chopped
	1 teaspoon salt
2 tablespoons instant or granular flour	¼ teaspoon white pepper
	1 recipe pie crust (or mix) for 2-crust, 9-inch pie
1 tablespoon dry vermouth	2 eggs

Preheat oven to 350°. Heat mushroom soup and gradually stir in flour. Cook for an additional 5 minutes, stirring constantly. Remove from fire and add vermouth. Set aside to cool slightly. In a bowl combine salmon, grated onion, chopped hard-boiled egg, soup mixture, salt and pepper. Roll out pie crust as thin as possible. With a sharp knife trim the dough into an even rectangular shape. Place the fish mixture across the lower half of the rectangle, the long way. Fold the short ends in and roll up like a jelly roll. Place on a buttered cookie pan with the seam side down. Beat the eggs well and brush the roll with the beaten eggs. Let dry for 5 minutes and brush again. Make 4 slits in the crust and bake for 1 hour or until very brown. Serves 6 as a luncheon dish.

Steward's Salmon

1 lb. can red salmon	dash pepper
½ pint sour cream	½ teaspoon dill weed
1 tablespoon lemon juice	½ medium unpeeled cucumber, sliced thin
1 tablespoon dry white wine	
½ teaspoon salt	1 medium onion, sliced thin

Drain salmon, reserving 2 tablespoons of the liquid. Break salmon into large pieces and put into a greased casserole. Mix salmon liquid, sour cream, lemon juice, wine, salt, pepper and dill weed together and pour over salmon. Place cucumbers over salmon. Top with sliced onions. Bake in a 350° oven for 30 minutes. Serves 3.

CHAPTER TWO

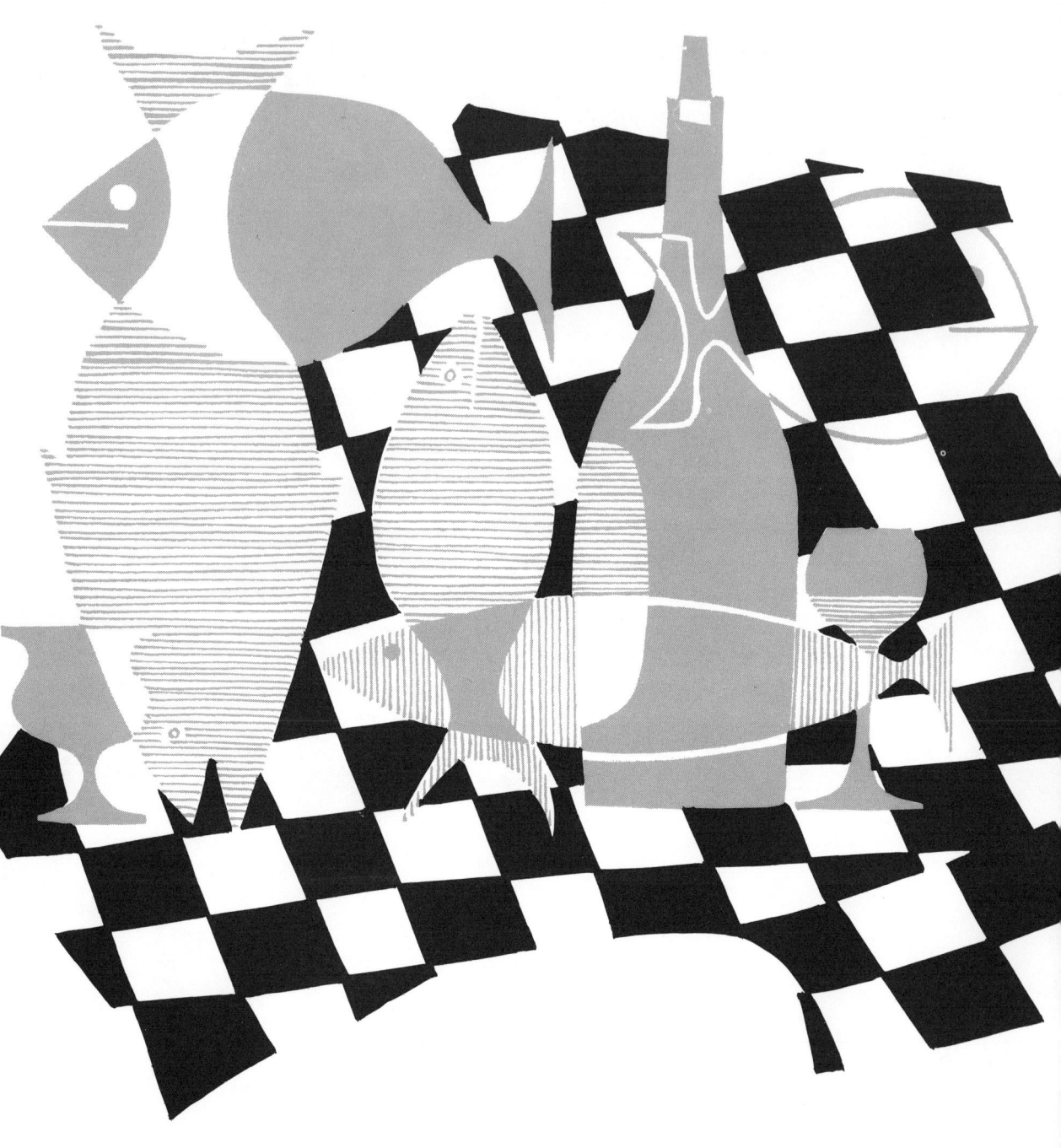

NAME YOUR POISSON

Sole Daiquiri

6 pieces fillet of sole
1 can frozen daiquiri mix
1 tablespoon light rum
2 tablespoons soy sauce
2 tablespoons peanut oil
1 teaspoon salt
1 recipe Ripe Olive Sauce

Defrost daiquiri mix and blend with the rum. Cut fillets in pieces about 1½ inches square and marinate in the liquid for 2 hours. Turn occasionally so that all sides are covered. Combine soy sauce, oil and salt. Drain fish from marinade, spread out on a broiling pan and brush with the soy mixture. Bake in a 450° oven until brown. Turn, brush again and brown other side. Place in a shallow serving pan and keep in a warm place while preparing the Ripe Olive Sauce. Pour sauce over fish and serve. Serves 6.

Ripe Olive Sauce

2 green onions, chopped
2 tablespoons butter or margarine
½ teaspoon soy sauce
1 tablespoon instant or granular flour
1 4½-oz. can chopped ripe olives
1 cup chablis

Melt butter, add green onions and cook for 3 minutes. Gradually stir in flour and cook for another 2 minutes and add the remaining ingredients, stirring all the time. Cook until very hot and slightly thickened.

Fillet of Sole With Grapes

8 pieces fillet of sole
    (approximately 2 lbs.)
½ teaspoon salt
¼ teaspoon white pepper
6 shallots, chopped
2 tablespoons butter or
    margarine
½ cup dry white wine
2 cups fresh seedless green
    grapes

Salt and pepper fish and lay flat. Divide shallots evenly over the fillets. Roll each fillet and secure with a toothpick. Melt butter in skillet. Add fish carefully and pour wine over fish. Add grapes, cover and cook over low heat for 10–12 minutes or until fish is done. Serve with sauce. Serves 4.

Sole Saturnalia

4 pieces fillet of sole
1 qt. champagne
1 teaspoon salt
1¼ cups Mornay Sauce
1 oz. caviar
2 truffles, sliced thin

Preheat oven to 350° and have all ingredients close at hand. Poach the fish in the champagne, using a shallow earthenware pan suitable for serving. Draw off (with a spoon or bulb baster) as much liquid as possible and set aside. Keep fish in a warm place. Make Mornay Sauce. Sprinkle fish with salt and then cover completely with the sauce. Return to oven for 10 minutes. Decorate with caviar and truffles. Serves 4.

Mornay Sauce

2 tablespoons butter
2 tablespoons flour
½ cup cream
½ cup poaching liquid
¼ teaspoon salt
⅛ teaspoon white pepper
⅛ teaspoon paprika
2 tablespoons butter
2 tablespoons each grated Parmesan and Swiss cheese

Melt 2 tablespoons butter over low heat and blend in flour. Slowly stir in cream and poaching liquid. Add seasonings. Keep stirring, and when hot add the rest of the butter and the cheeses. Continue stirring until cheese is melted.

Abbé's Sole

4 pieces fillet of sole
1 package frozen asparagus spears
¼ lb. mushrooms, sliced
¼ green pepper, chopped
1 small onion, chopped
2 tablespoons butter or margarine
1 can cream of celery soup
1 teaspoon Worcestershire sauce
1 teaspoon lemon juice
1 tablespoon dry sherry
½ teaspoon salt
¼ teaspoon pepper
3 tablespoons grated Parmesan cheese

Parboil asparagus until they are underdone and firm. While vegetable is cooking, sauté mushrooms, pepper and onions in butter until onions are golden. Slowly add soup, stirring constantly until smooth. Add Worcestershire, lemon juice and sherry. Stir well. Salt and pepper fish and lay flat for stuffing. Divide asparagus equally onto each fillet. Wrap fish around asparagus and lay in a greased shallow pan. Pour sauce over fish. Sprinkle with Parmesan cheese. Bake in a 350° oven for 20 minutes. Serves 4.

Vintner's Sole

6 pieces fillet of sole, bass or flounder
2 cups dry white wine
3 cups fresh bread crumbs
½ cup butter
1 teaspoon salt
dash white pepper
1 8-oz. can minced clams with juice
2 cups canned tomatoes, drained and chopped

Marinate fish in wine for 2 hours. Remove from wine and drain well. Place on a large buttered baking-and-serving pan. Cook bread crumbs in the butter. Salt and pepper the fillets. Arrange the clams over the fish. Then pour the tomatoes over all. Sprinkle with a little additional salt. Cover with the buttered crumbs and bake 25 minutes in a 375° oven. Serves 6.

The Innkeeper's Sole

6 serving-size pieces fillet of sole
3 tablespoons butter, melted
2 tablespoons dry white wine
½ lemon
½ teaspoon salt
¼ teaspoon pepper
6 tablespoons bread crumbs
½ pint sour cream
2 teaspoons anchovy paste
parsley

Lay fish in a shallow greased baking dish so that the pieces do not overlap. Drizzle the fish with melted butter and wine. Squeeze the lemon over fish. Season with salt and pepper and sprinkle 1 tablespoon bread crumbs over each fillet. Bake in a 350° oven for 15 minutes or until done. While fish is cooking, put sour cream into a small bowl and whip with a fork until it is fluffy and creamy. Add anchovy paste and mix well. Arrange the fish on a platter, garnish with parsley and serve anchovy sauce separately. Serves 6.

Sole Marsala

8 pieces fillet of sole
2 cups cooked lobster meat
½ cup dry white wine
1 teaspoon salt
¼ teaspoon pepper
1 teaspoon chervil
3 egg yolks

2 tablespoons cream
1 tablespoon tarragon vinegar
1 tablespoon marsala
4 tablespoons butter or margarine
½ cup cooked chopped spinach, well drained

Place fillets in lightly greased baking dish. Pour wine over fish and sprinkle with ½ teaspoon salt, pepper and chervil. Cover fish with foil and bake in a 350° oven for 15 minutes. While fish is cooking, make the sauce. In a double boiler, over simmering water, combine egg yolks, cream, vinegar and ¼ teaspoon salt. Beat with a whisk until sauce thickens. Remove from heat. In a skillet toss chunks of lobster into hot melted butter and add marsala. Take fish from oven and transfer to a shallow casserole. Scatter lobster on fish. Finish sauce by adding lobster butter, cooked spinach and any fish juices that remain, stirring constantly with a whisk. Cook slowly and continue stirring. Taste and add last ¼ teaspoon salt if necessary. Pour sauce over fish and put under broiler until lightly browned. Serves 8.

Name Your Poisson

Sole Curacao

4 large pieces fillet of sole
4 tablespoons oil
6 small green onions, thinly sliced
½ lb. fresh mushrooms, sliced
¼ teaspoon salt
⅛ teaspoon pepper
¼ teaspoon MSG powder or Accent
1 teaspoon soy sauce
½ cup dry white wine
¼ cup orange juice
3 tablespoons Curacao or Grand Marnier
2 tablespoons minced or chopped parsley
paprika

Put 2 tablespoons oil in the bottom of a flat baking dish. Cover bottom with half of the onions and mushrooms. Salt and pepper the fish lightly. Lay fish on onions and mushrooms. Sprinkle fish with soy sauce and MSG powder. Add rest of oil and vegetables, wine, orange juice and Curacao. Salt and pepper again very lightly. Bake in a 350° oven uncovered for 30 minutes. Garnish with parsley and paprika. Serves 4.

Sole on Tap

4 pieces fillet of sole
1¼ cups flour
1 cup cornstarch
1 teaspoon salt
1 can beer
4 egg whites, beaten stiff
3 cups oil for frying

Combine flour, cornstarch, salt and beer thoroughly. Beat egg whites very stiff and fold into the mixture. Let batter stand at room temperature for 6 hours. Cut fillets in quarters and dry thoroughly with paper towels. Heat oil in a small deep pan until a

1-inch cube of bread browns in 1 minute. Dip pieces of fish in the stiff batter and fry a few at a time until golden and puffy. Keep warm until all the pieces are fried. Serve with Anchovy Mayonnaise. Serves 4.

Anchovy Mayonnaise

1 cup mayonnaise
2 anchovy fillets, mashed
¼ cup lemon juice

Combine all ingredients. Can be prepared in advance.

Demon Rum Sole

2 lbs. fillet of sole
¾ cup oil
3 cloves garlic, mashed
3 teaspoons chopped dried mint leaves
1½ teaspoons chili powder
3 teaspoons sweet basil
2 tablespoons vinegar
1 tablespoon light rum
1 tablespoon lemon juice
½ teaspoon salt
¼ teaspoon pepper
3 teaspoons turmeric

Combine all ingredients except fish and mix well. Add the fish and gently mix again. Marinate at least 2 hours. Put the fish and marinade in a shallow pan and broil 9 minutes. Serve with rice. Pour pan juices over fish. Serves 4.

Sole Chablis

3 lbs. fillet of sole
2 tablespoons butter or margarine
1 pint sour cream
1 jar marinated artichoke hearts, drained and thinly sliced
½ cup chablis
6 heaping tablespoons Parmesan cheese
¼ teaspoon paprika
½ teaspoon salt
¼ teaspoon pepper
2 tablespoons oil
½ lemon or lime

Melt butter and add sour cream slowly, stirring constantly. Add artichoke hearts, wine, cheese and paprika. Stir well until smooth. Lay fish in a shallow pan. Salt and pepper fish and drizzle a little oil over each piece. Squeeze lemon or lime over the fish. Place in a 350° oven and bake 10–15 minutes. Place fish on a large warm serving platter and pour hot sauce over fish. Serve immediately. Serves 6.

Bootlegger's Sole

1 thin piece fillet of sole, approximately 1 lb.
3 tablespoons butter
½ teaspoon salt
¼ teaspoon pepper
⅓ cup coarsely chopped fresh mushrooms
⅓ cup chopped fresh parsley
½ teaspoon oregano
juice of ½ lemon
2 tablespoons dry vermouth

Grease shallow baking pan with 1 tablespoon butter. Salt and pepper fish and lay flat for stuffing. Mix mushrooms, parsley and oregano and spread on fish. Roll like a jelly roll and tie in 3 places

with string. Place in a baking pan. Pour lemon juice and vermouth over fish. Dot with remaining butter. Bake in a 375° oven for 20 minutes or until fish is done. Baste frequently. Before serving, remove string. Serves 3.

Sole on a Bender

2 lbs. fillet of sole
1 tablespoon butter or margarine
1 medium onion, sliced thin
1 small can chopped mushrooms
½ teaspoon salt
¼ teaspoon white pepper
1 can lobster bisque
1 tablespoon dry sherry

Rub the bottom of a shallow baking dish with the butter. Put the onions on bottom of dish and mushrooms on top of the onions.

Name Your Poisson 51

Arrange fish on top of mushrooms and sprinkle with salt and pepper. Mix soup with sherry and pour over fish. Bake in a 350° oven for 30 minutes. Serves 6.

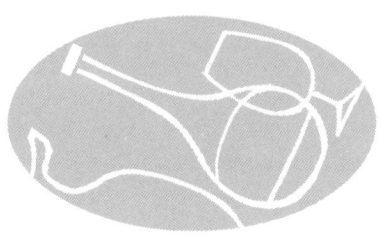

Wino's Sole Amandine

2 lbs. fillet of sole, halibut or any other broiling fish
¼ teaspoon salt
¼ teaspoon pepper
½ teaspoon seasoned salt
juice of ½ lemon

3 tablespoons butter or margarine
2 tablespoons dry white wine
⅓ cup slivered almonds

Place fish in a greased baking pan and season with salt, pepper, seasoned salt and lemon juice. Let stand for about 20 minutes. Dot with about 1 tablespoon butter. Broil about 8 minutes or until almost done and just turning light brown. While fish is broiling, melt remaining butter in a small saucepan. Add wine and almonds for a few minutes. When fish is almost done, spoon butter, wine and almond sauce over fish and broil until golden brown. Do not let almonds get too brown. Baste the fish with the pan juices. Serves 4.

Sole Vin du Pays

2 lbs. fillet of sole
½ teaspoon salt
¼ teaspoon white pepper
1 cup dry white wine

1 can frozen cream of
  shrimp soup
¼ lb. tiny cooked shrimp
  (optional)

Season fish with salt and pepper and place in a greased casserole. Pour wine over fish so that fish is covered. You may need more wine. Cover casserole and bake in a 400° oven for 10 minutes or until fish is done. While fish is cooking, heat shrimp soup, stirring until hot and smooth. Remove fish to a serving platter. Pour 1 cup liquid from casserole into soup and mix well. Discard remaining liquid. Pour over fish and garnish with tiny shrimp. Serves 6.

Bourbon Street Fish Roll

4 small pieces fillet of sole
4 small pieces fillet of salmon
8 medium size shrimp,
  cooked and shelled
4 tablespoons parsley,
  chopped

1 can cream of asparagus
  soup, undiluted
2 tablespoons dry sherry

Make fish rolls so that shrimp are in the center. Wrap the salmon on one side of the shrimp. Wrap the sole on the other side. These fish will overlap. Distribute the parsley on one side of the roll between the salmon and the sole. Secure the rolls with a string. Put the fish rolls in a greased baking pan. Cover with the soup blended with wine. Bake in a 400° oven for 20 minutes or until done. Serves 4.

Double, Sole and Crab

6 large serving pieces fillet of sole	1½ cups milk or light cream
12 Dungeness crab legs, about 2½ inches long, cooked and shelled, or ½ lb. crabmeat	¼ cup dry sherry
	3 heaping tablespoons mayonnaise
½ teaspoon salt	¼ teaspoon salt
½ teaspoon seasoned salt	dash of pepper
3 tablespoons butter or margarine	1 drop Tabasco sauce
	dash of curry powder
3 tablespoons flour	3 tablespoons Parmesan cheese

Season the sole with salt and seasoned salt. Wrap the sole around the crab legs or crabmeat and lay the stuffed sole carefully in a shallow casserole. Make sauce by melting the butter, adding the flour and mixing until smooth. Slowly add the milk and stir constantly until the sauce is thick and creamy. Add sherry. Be sure mayonnaise is at room temperature. Whip it with a spoon until it is light and fluffy and add it to the sauce, mixing thoroughly. Add the salt, pepper, drop of Tabasco and dash of curry powder. Mix again and pour the sauce over the fish. Sprinkle with grated Parmesan cheese. Bake in a 350° oven for 30 minutes or until fish is done. Serves 6.

Loaded Sole

2 lbs. fillet of sole	½ teaspoon sweet basil
1 small can salmon	1 bunch green grapes or small can white grapes
1 can cream of onion soup	
¼ cup dry white wine	

Cut sole into 8 pieces. Wrap some of the canned salmon in each piece of sole and skewer with a toothpick. Mix soup, wine, sweet basil and grapes together. Put fish in a greased casserole. Pour sauce over fish. Bake in a 350° oven for 30 minutes. Serves 4.

Sole Cave du Vin

2 lbs. fillet of sole
3 large onions, coarsely chopped
2–3 tablespoons oil
½ lb. mushrooms, sliced
½ pint sour cream
1 can tomato soup
2 tablespoons Burgundy

Fry the onions in oil until they are yellow and transparent. Add the mushrooms and sauté until the onions are almost brown. Mix the sour cream and tomato soup. Add wine. Add onions and mushrooms and stir. Cut fish into 2 by 5-inch lengths. Roll each piece and place upright, closely packed, in a casserole. Pour sauce over fish and bake in a 350° oven for 30 minutes. Serves 6.

Flounder Up Tight

8 pieces fillet of flounder
1 can cream of mushroom soup
1 teaspoon Angostura bitters
4 oz. chopped canned mushrooms
½ lb. tiny cooked shrimp
1 teaspoon salt
dash white pepper
½ cup bread crumbs
2 tablespoons butter or margarine
2 tablespoons chopped parsley

Coil each fillet inside a buttered muffin cup and place the muffin pan on a foil-lined cookie sheet. Into the center of the fillets add the next 6 ingredients combined. Sprinkle tops with buttered bread crumbs. Bake 30 minutes in a 350° oven. Remove from cups carefully with a curved spoon and garnish with parsley. Serve with buttered rice. Serves 8.

Fried Sand Dabs

4 sand dabs
½ teaspoon salt
¼ teaspoon pepper
4 tablespoons oil
1 tablespoon flour
juice of 1 lemon
1 tablespoon dry white wine
1 tablespoon parsley
⅛ teaspoon thyme

There are two simple ways to prepare sand dabs. One is to season them lightly with salt and pepper, flour generously and fry quickly on both sides in hot butter and oil. Serve with plenty of lemon. Another way to prepare them takes the ingredients listed above. Salt and pepper the sand dabs on both sides and place on a flat pan with 2 tablespoons oil. Sprinkle with flour. Put the pan in a

450° oven. Mix the lemon juice, wine and rest of oil, parsley and thyme. Baste the sand dabs with this mixture frequently. Bake 20–30 minutes. Just before serving, brown in the broiler. Serves 2.

Tavern Sand Dabs

8 sand dabs
¼ cup flour
1 teaspoon salt
½ teaspoon pepper
oil for frying
2 green onions, thinly sliced
4 tablespoons fresh parsley, chopped
⅛ teaspoon marjoram
1 lemon, sliced thin
½ cup dry white wine
1 3-oz. can chopped mushrooms
2 tablespoons slivered almonds

Heat oil in skillet. Combine flour, salt and pepper in a plastic bag. Add fish to the bag, a few at a time, and shake to coat. Brown sand dabs in oil 2 minutes on each side. You may have to do this in two or three batches. Don't crowd the fish while it is frying. Discard excess oil. Place all the fish and remaining ingredients in pan. Cover the skillet and cook for 10 minutes. Serves 4.

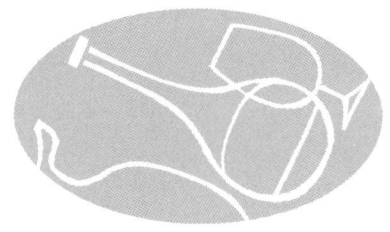

CHAPTER THREE

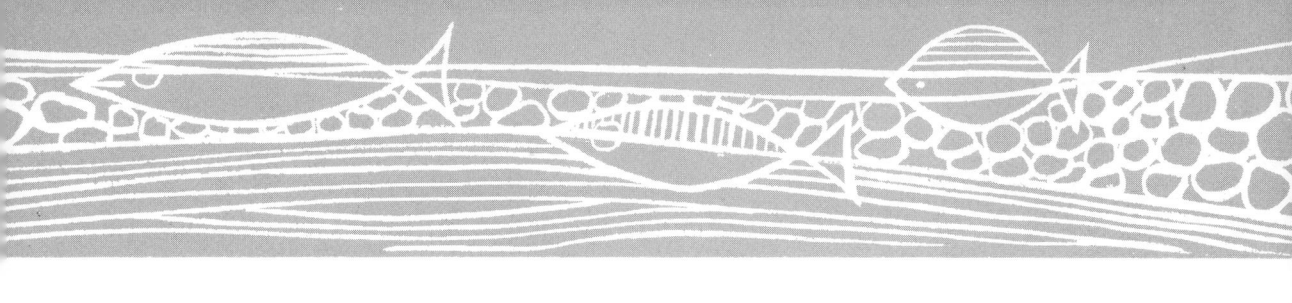

Winemaster's Snapper

4 slices red snapper
½ teaspoon salt
¼ teaspoon pepper
juice of ½ lemon
¼ cup dry white wine
4 teaspoons Worcestershire sauce
4 slices bacon

Sprinkle each slice with lemon juice, wine, salt and pepper. Line broiler pan with aluminum foil. Add fish. Sprinkle the fish with Worcestershire sauce. Put one strip of bacon on each steak. Bake in a 400° oven for 30 minutes. Discard the bacon. Remove from oven. If fish is not brown, finish cooking under broiler for 2–3 minutes. Serves 4.

Sweet Sherry Snapper

1 2–3 lb. piece of red snapper
½ cup peanut oil
3 cloves garlic, minced
¼ teaspoon salt
dash white pepper
2 tablespoons soy sauce
⅓ cup sweet sherry
2 teaspoons fresh grated ginger
3 green onions, sliced lengthwise
1 bunch parsley
1 jar marinated artichokes, drained

Use a fairly large greased oven-proof pan. Place the fish in the pan. Combine all the other ingredients with the exception of the green onions, parsley and artichokes. Pour this mixture over the fish. Lay the long strips of green onions over the fish and cover tightly with heavy aluminum foil. Steam in a 350° oven for 30 minutes. Uncover and carefully lift the fish onto a warm platter. Strain the pan liquid over the fish. Decorate with parsley and artichoke hearts. Serve immediately. Serves 4.

Off the Deep End

Brandy Snappers

4 pieces red snapper	8 brandied apricots
½ teaspoon salt	2 tablespoons apricot brandy
2 cups cooked rice	2 tablespoons chopped
4 tablespoons butter	cashew nuts

Sprinkle the fish with salt, place it in a baking-and-serving pan, and broil for 10 minutes at 400°. Remove from broiler and reduce heat to 325°. Border the pan with the rice and dot fish and rice with butter. Return to oven for 5 minutes. Heat apricots in juice. Discard juice. Remove from oven and sprinkle the brandy over the fish. Nestle the apricots in the rice border. Sprinkle cashews over all. Serve immediately. Serves 4.

Neptune's Harvest

2 lbs. red snapper, cut in 2-inch pieces	½ cup chopped parsley
1 cup dry white wine	3 shallots, sliced
½ teaspoon salt	juice of 2 lemons
¼ teaspoon freshly ground pepper	½ lb. fresh mushrooms, stems removed
1 tablespoon oil	8 large raw shrimp, shelled

Put wine in bottom of large skillet. Salt and pepper fish and rub with oil. Add to wine. Add parsley, shallots, lemon juice and mushrooms. Cover pan and cook on low heat for about 8 minutes or until fish is done. Add shrimp and cook for a few minutes longer until shrimp turn pink. Serve with lots of French bread. Serves 4.

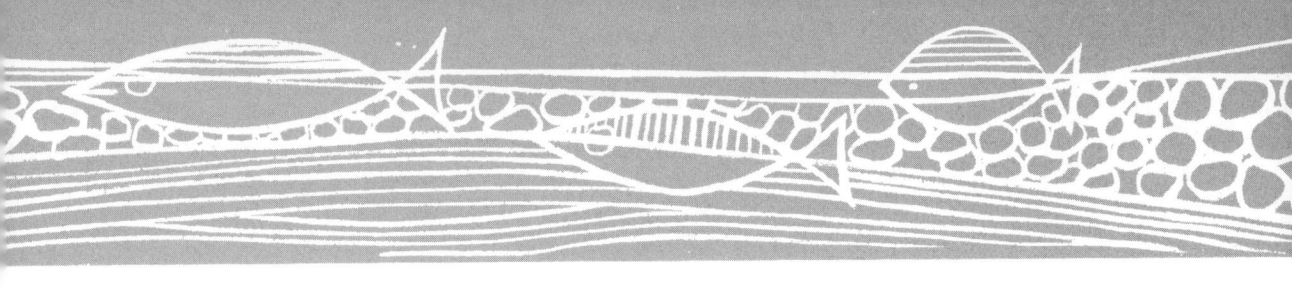

Snapper Olé

4 slices red snapper
1 recipe or package of
  Spanish rice for 4 servings
½ teaspoon salt
¼ teaspoon pepper
pinch sweet basil
1 lemon, sliced

1 8-oz. can chopped clams,
  drained
3 cups canned tomatoes,
  drained and chopped
½ cup dry red wine
½ cup Parmesan cheese

Prepare Spanish rice and spread in buttered casserole. Add fish. Sprinkle with salt, pepper and sweet basil. Place clams and lemon over fish and add tomatoes. Pour wine over all. Sprinkle with Parmesan cheese. Bake in a 350° oven for 25 minutes. Serves 4.

Corking Good Red Snapper

2 lbs. fillet of red snapper
2 large stalks celery, sliced in
  ½-inch pieces
1 medium onion, sliced
2 tablespoons oil
1 teaspoon salt
½ teaspoon pepper

¼ teaspoon celery seed
1 small green pepper,
  cut in strips
1 can cream of celery soup
2 tablespoons dry white wine
2 tablespoons chopped parsley

Sauté onion, celery and half of the salt and pepper in oil until onion is golden. Put fish in a shallow baking dish. Season with remaining salt and pepper. Sprinkle celery seed over fish. Arrange green pepper strips over fish and surround fish with onions and celery. Mix soup and wine and pour over fish. Bake in a 350° oven for 30 minutes. Sprinkle with chopped parsley. Serves 6.

Off the Deep End

Codfish Down the Hatch

1½ lbs. pieces ling cod or black cod	1 bay leaf
1 carrot	1 tablespoon raw or brown sugar
2 stalks celery	2 teaspoons arrowroot or cornstarch
small ball parsley root	¼ cup water
½ green pepper	handful parsley, chopped
¼ cup wine vinegar	1 tablespoon butter or margarine
2 cups water	24 Malaga, purple or black Italian grapes, pitted
½ cup dry white wine	
5 peppercorns, white preferably	

Chop carrot, celery, parsley root and green pepper. Put vegetables, vinegar, water, wine, bay leaf, peppercorns and sugar in a large skillet or Dutch oven. Simmer until vegetables are tender. Add serving-size pieces of fish and turn heat down to a slow simmer. When the fish is done, remove from pan and keep warm. To the pan, add the arrowroot dissolved in the ¼ cup water, and thicken broth, stirring constantly. When it is thick and transparent, add parsley, butter and the grapes. Pour over the fish and serve immediately. Serves 4.

Fillets, Coup de Vin

2 lbs. cod fillets	1 cup sour cream
¼ lb. bleu cheese, mashed	1 cup dry white wine

Put fillets in a greased baking pan. Mix bleu cheese, sour cream and wine until well blended. Pour over fish and bake in a 400° oven for 25 minutes. Serves 6.

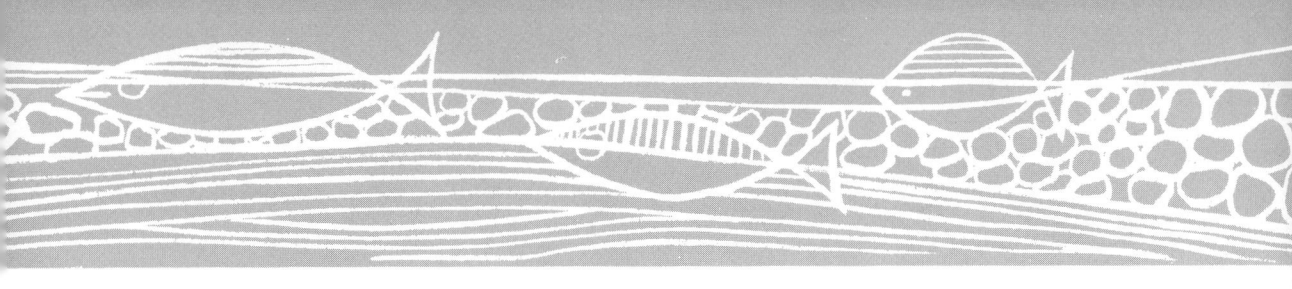

Black Cod Bouzo

1 2-lb. piece black cod
½ teaspoon salt
¼ teaspoon pepper
1 medium onion, sliced
1 large clove garlic, slivered
4 tablespoons butter or margarine
2 tablespoons ouzo or dry white wine
½ green pepper, sliced
12 Greek olives
8 lemon wedges

Arrange the cod in a greased shallow pan. Salt and pepper the cod. Arrange onion slices and garlic on fish. Dot with butter. Broil 8–10 minutes or until done, basting frequently with the pan juices to which you have added the wine and more butter if necessary. Remove to serving dish and garnish with green pepper, Greek olives and lemon wedges. Serves 4.

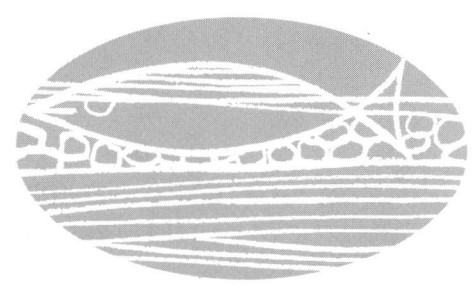

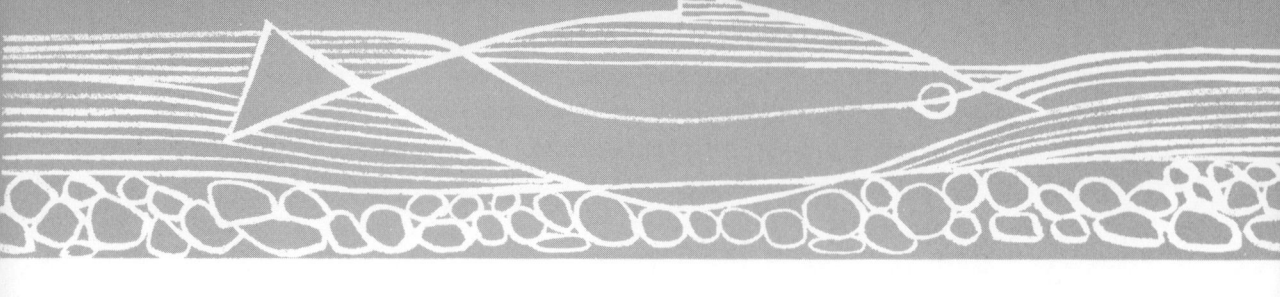

Old-Fashioned Fish and Jelly

2 lbs. pike
2 onions, sliced
2 stalks celery, sliced
3 carrots, sliced
½ teaspoon salt
¼ teaspoon coarse ground pepper
3 large potatoes
¼ cup dry white wine
parsley

Slice the pike into 5 or 6 serving pieces. Put the onions, celery and carrots in a big pot. Place the fish on the vegetables. Add just enough water to cover the fish. Add the salt and pepper. Cook the fish for 20–25 minutes until done on a low, low flame. While the fish is cooking, peel the potatoes and cook them in salted water until they are done but still firm. Lift the fish out of the pot very carefully and place on a deep serving platter. Slice the potatoes about ½ inch thick and place them around the fish. Next, take the carrots out of the pot and put some in a decorative manner on each piece of fish. Strain the liquid in which the fish has been cooked, add wine and pour over the fish. Rearrange the potatoes and carrots if necessary. The bouillon should cover the fish and potatoes. Cool and refrigerate overnight. The bouillon will have jellied. Garnish with parsley. This is a main dish course with salad and lots of good bread. Or, if you are having a formal dinner, this makes a delightful fish course. Serves 5–6.

No Pain Pike

6 pike or halibut fillets
1 12-oz. can or bottle clam juice
2 egg yolks
1 tablespoon dry vermouth
¼ teaspoon salt
dash white pepper
1 tablespoon butter
1 lemon, sliced

Slowly poach fillets in clam juice for 20 minutes. Lift out carefully with a slotted spoon and place on paper towels for a moment and then transfer to a serving dish and keep warm. Beat egg yolks well, and add vermouth, salt and pepper. Gradually add the hot clam juice, beating constantly. Reheat slowly, add butter and stir. Pour over the fish and decorate with sliced lemon. Serves 6.

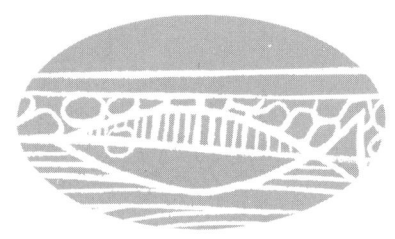

Cellar Pike

4 thick slices pike
enough dry white wine to cover fish
1 can flat anchovies, drained
1 tablespoon capers
6 shallots, minced
4 tablespoons butter

In a large flat skillet that can go from stove to the table, poach the fish in wine for 15 minutes. With a large spoon or bulb baster, draw off all but a very small amount of the wine into a small pan. Cover the fish slices with the anchovies, capers and shallots and dot with 2 tablespoons of the butter. Place in a 325° oven for 10 minutes. Reduce the cooking wine to about ½ cup. Add the remaining butter and bring to a boil. Pour over the fish and serve immediately. Serves 4.

Stuffed Barracuda, Patron

1 4-lb. piece of barracuda	1 8-oz. can minced clams, drained
½ cup chopped onion	1 cup fresh bean sprouts
4 tablespoons butter or margarine	2 tablespoons dry white wine
2 tablespoons dried parsley	6 strips bacon
1 cup bread crumbs, fresh or dried	salt
	pepper

Sauté onion in butter until brown. Add parsley, bread crumbs, clams, bean sprouts and wine. Mix thoroughly and taste for seasoning. Add salt and pepper if necessary. Stuff fish with the dressing. Place bacon strips on top of fish. Tie with string in several places and put into a baking dish that is lined with cheesecloth. Bake uncovered in a 350° oven for 1 hour. Baste occasionally with pan juices. Use the cheesecloth to transfer the fish to a serving platter. Pour the pan juices over fish. Serves 6.

Apricot Sour Trout

6 small trout	1 teaspoon salt
½ cup apricot nectar	¼ teaspoon pepper
juice of 1 lemon	¼ teaspoon paprika
2 tablespoons almonds, pulverized in blender	1 cup flour
	oil for frying
1 teaspoon grated orange rind	2 tablespoons butter
1 teaspoon grated lemon rind	3 tablespoons apricot brandy

Wash and dry trout. Combine apricot nectar and lemon juice and brush both sides of each fish. Combine next 7 ingredients in a plastic bag, shaking them all together thoroughly. Drop 1 fish at a time into the flour mixture and coat completely. Repeat until all the fish are covered with the flour mixture. Heat the oil until very hot and fry the fish. Do not put too many in the pan, as the fish should get crisp very quickly. While fish are frying, melt the butter in a small pan and stir in the apricot brandy. Remove the hot fish to a warm serving platter and pour the brandy butter over them. Serves 6.

Trout With a Bun On

4 small trout
3 tablespoons butter
1 loaf French bread, unsliced
½ cup melted butter
¼ teaspoon garlic salt
2 tablespoons butter
2 teaspoons shallots, minced
½ teaspoon salt
¾ cup fresh bread crumbs
3 tablespoons dry red wine

Cut bread all the way across into 2 long halves and then cut each of these in half in the opposite direction to give you 4 rectangular pieces. With your fingers tear out most of the soft inside bread and set aside. Brush insides of crust with the ½ cup of melted butter and sprinkle with garlic salt. Place on a cookie sheet and bake in a 375° oven for 5 minutes or until light brown. Sauté the trout in the 3 tablespoons of butter for 6 minutes on each side, or until a golden color. Place 1 trout in each bread shell and keep in a warm place. To the skillet add the 2 tablespoons butter, shallots and salt. Cook 1 minute. Add bread crumbs (that have been made in the blender) and cook for an additional 2 minutes. Stir in the wine and heat. Pour over the trout and serve immediately. Serves 4.

Distiller's Trout

4 very small trout
6 tablespoons butter
1 cup cooked rice
½ cup tiny cooked shrimp
1 tablespoon fresh chives
   or chopped green onions

4 large mushroom caps
½ teaspoon salt
¼ teaspoon white pepper
¼ cup heavy cream
2 tablespoons bourbon

Sauté trout in butter just enough to brown them. Cut four pieces heavy aluminum foil into 8-inch squares. In each square place 1 trout, ¼ cup rice, a fourth of the shrimp, 1 mushroom cap and chives, salt and pepper. To the skillet in which the trout was cooked, add the cream and heat thoroughly. Remove from heat and add bourbon. Divide this mixture into the four foil squares. Fold the foil around the ingredients and seal firmly into neat packages. Place on a baking pan in a 425° oven for 15 minutes. To serve, place package on individual dinner plates and let each person tear open the foil. Serves 4.

Bar Fly Trout

1 3-lb. trout
½ cup finely chopped onion
½ cup finely chopped celery
½ cup finely chopped carrots
3 tablespoons melted butter
½ cup dry red wine

½ teaspoon salt
¼ teaspoon pepper
2 tablespoons butter
½ teaspoon tomato paste
2 tablespoons dry red wine

In a shallow oven-to-table baking pan place a layer of all the vegetables. Pour melted butter over the vegetables, then place the fish over them. Pour the ½ cup of wine around the fish and sprinkle with salt and pepper. Cover with heavy aluminum foil and bake in a 375° oven for 20 minutes. While fish is baking, melt the remaining butter, stir in tomato paste and 2 tablespoons of wine. Remove fish from oven, uncover and increase heat to 450°. Place fish under broiler for 2 minutes, Remove from oven and spoon the tomato and wine sauce over the fish. Serves 4.

Truite aux Boites

1 3-lb. trout
½ cup sauterne
⅛ teaspoon coarse black pepper
¼ teaspoon salt
¼ teaspoon garlic salt
¼ teaspoon seasoned salt
1 large lime, sliced thin
1 medium onion, sliced thin
4 tablespoons butter or margarine

Remove head and tail of trout and lay in a shallow baking dish. Pour wine over fish. Sprinkle with seasonings. Fill cavity of fish with 3 or 4 lime and onion slices. Place rest of lime on fish and cover with onions. Put rest of onions around fish. Dot with butter. Cover with aluminum foil and bake in a 400° oven for 20 minutes. Uncover and bake for another 20 minutes. Baste frequently. Serves 4.

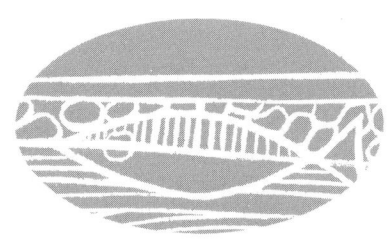

CHAPTER FOUR

Mahimahi on the Town in Kauai

6 slices mahimahi
1 teaspoon salt
½ teaspoon pepper
8 tablespoons butter or margarine
juice of ½ lemon
½ cup slivered almonds
¼ lb. tiny cooked shrimp
2 tablespoons chablis

Mahimahi comes from the seas around Hawaii, but more and more it can be found in the frozen fish department of the supermarkets. Salt and pepper the mahimahi and place it in a baking dish. Dot with half of the butter and a mere squirt of lemon. Broil until lightly browned. In a small saucepan, melt the remaining butter. Add the lemon juice, almonds and tiny shrimp. Cook only until the shrimp are heated. Add wine. Then spoon the shrimp and almonds over the mahimahi. Pour the butter sauce over all and broil for a minute or two longer. Serve with rice or French fried potatoes. Serves 6.

Island Binge

4 slices mahimahi
2 tablespoons butter
8 thick slices oranges
2 tablespoons Curacao
1 recipe Curry Sauce

Lay fish in a single layer on a buttered baking-and-serving pan, using all the butter. Cover the fish with curry sauce. Bake in a 350° oven for 20 minutes. Peel and slice oranges. Remove pan from oven. Make a border of the oranges and drizzle the Curacao over them. Return to the oven for an additional 5 minutes. Serve immediately. Serves 4.

Stewed to the Gills

Curry Sauce

2 tablespoons butter
1 tablespoon onion, chopped
2 tablespoons flour
1 cup clam juice
1 teaspoon curry powder
¼ cup heavy cream

Cook chopped onion in butter until golden and limp. Stir in flour. Keep stirring and gradually add clam juice. Cook until thick, then add curry powder and slowly add cream, stirring constantly. Cook again until thick.

Whitefish, Crème Sauterne

3 lbs. fillet of whitefish, butterfish or red snapper
3 tablespoons butter or margarine
3 large onions, sliced thin
½ cup sauterne
1 lb. mushrooms, sliced
juice of 1 lemon
½ teaspoon salt
¼ teaspoon pepper
Crème Sauterne

Melt the butter in a frying pan. Add the onion and wine. Cover and cook over low heat until the onions are transparent, but not browned. Put onions and any liquid in the bottom of a large flat casserole. Add sliced mushrooms. Lay fish over mushrooms and add lemon juice, salt and pepper. Spoon Crème Sauterne over fish. Place in a 350° oven for 30 minutes. Serves 6-8.

Crème Sauterne

1½ cups mayonnaise
¾ cup sour cream
1 tablespoon lemon juice
1 tablespoon sauterne
½ teaspoon salt
¼ teaspoon white pepper
¼ teaspoon paprika

Have all ingredients at room temperature. Mix thoroughly.

Whitefish Prosit!

1 4-lb. piece whitefish
8 small potatoes
2 teaspoons salt
½ teaspoon pepper
1 pint sour cream, room temperature
⅓ cup chopped chives
3 tablespoons oil
¼ cup riesling

Cook peeled potatoes until done but firm. Cool slightly and slice in ¼-inch slices. Season the potatoes with half of the salt and pepper. Mix sour cream and and chives. Combine the potatoes with half of the sour cream mixture. While potatoes are cooling, put oil in the bottom of a large baking dish (larger than necessary for just the fish). Place fish in center of dish. Spoon some of the oil on fish. Pour wine over fish and add remainder of salt and pepper. Broil in a 450° oven for 20 minutes or until fish is done. Surround fish with potatoes mixed with sour cream. Put under broiler for 2 minutes. To serve, spoon rest of sour cream and chives over fish. Serves 8.

Stewed to the Gills

Fish and Sweet Potatoes L'Chayim

Not great

6 serving slices whitefish or black cod	2 onions, sliced thin
6 medium sweet potatoes	1 green pepper, coarsely diced
1 teaspoon salt	1 can tomato soup
½ teaspoon pepper	1 soup can of milk
4 stalks celery, sliced	¼ cup dry sherry
4 carrots, sliced thin	

Peel potatoes and cut them in half lengthwise. Place them in the bottom of an oblong baking dish. Place the fish on top of the potatoes. Salt and pepper with half of the seasonings. Distribute the vegetables over the fish and potatoes. Salt and pepper again. Mix soup, milk and sherry and pour over the fish and vegetables. Bake in a 350° oven for 1 hour or until potatoes are done. Baste occasionally. Serves 6.

Gimlet Fish

2 lbs. butterfish	1 3-oz. jar macadamia nuts, chopped
½ teaspoon salt	juice of 1 lime
¼ teaspoon pepper	⅓ cup gin
4 tablespoons butter	

Salt and pepper fish and put in broiling pan. Dot with 2 tablespoons butter and broil for 10 minutes or until done, basting once or twice. Melt rest of butter in a small skillet. Lightly brown nuts in butter, but do not brown the butter. Add lime juice and gin. Mix and continue cooking for 1 minute or until hot. When fish is done, remove to serving platter. Spoon wine sauce over fish. Serves 6.

Highball Butterfish

4 slices butterfish
juice of 1 lemon
1 teaspoon salt
1 tablespoon dry sherry

1 can frozen cream of shrimp soup
2 egg whites

Broil fillets for 10 minutes. Sprinkle with salt and lemon juice. While fish is broiling heat the undiluted soup and add the sherry. Beat egg whites very stiff. Remove fish from broiler, cover with the egg whites and pour soup mixture around the fish very carefully. Return to broiler for 2 minutes. Serve immediately. Serves 4.

Brass Rail Perch

6 perch
½ teaspoon salt
¼ teaspoon white pepper

6 tablespoons butter
3 tablespoons peanut oil

Season the perch. Heat butter and oil until very hot and sauté the fish about 4 minutes on each side or until brown. Set aside in a warm place. Serve with Cold Yogurt Sauce. Serves 6.

Cold Yogurt Sauce

1 cup chilled yogurt
2 tablespoons lemon juice
1 tablespoon dry vermouth

2 tablespoons chopped chives
1 teaspoon grated lemon rind
1 teaspoon chopped parsley

Combine all the ingredients and serve with hot fish. Can be made 2 hours ahead of time with no change in quality.

Stewed to the Gills

Public House Haddock

2 lbs. haddock fillets
2 medium onions, sliced
½ teaspoon salt
dash pepper
2 tablespoons chopped parsley
½ teaspoon marjoram
1 bay leaf, crushed
2 whole cloves
½ teaspoon caraway seeds
½ cup dried bread crumbs
1 can beer

Cover bottom of greased shallow casserole with onions. Salt and pepper fish lightly and lay over onions. Sprinkle with parsley, marjoram, bay leaf, cloves and caraway seeds. Sprinkle bread crumbs over all. Pour beer around fish. Bake in a 375° oven for 30 minutes or until fish is done. Serves 6.

Wholly Mackerel

1 3–4 lb. piece of mackerel or other firm fish suitable for stuffing
½ cup chopped parsley
½ cup chopped dill pickles
2 tablespoons oil
2 tablespoons dry white wine
½ teaspoon salt
¼ teaspoon pepper
18 wrinkled black or Greek olives

Mix parsley and pickles. Cover the bottom of a baking-and-serving pan with oil. Lay fish in pan, open cavity and stuff with pickles and parsley. Pour wine over fish. Sprinkle with salt and pepper. Place the Greek olives around the fish. Bake in a 400° oven for 30 minutes or until the fish is done. You can tell if it is done by gently flaking a little with a fork. Serves 6.

Orange Blossom

2 lbs. pompano, cut in serving pieces
3 medium oranges
¼ cup Grand Marnier
½ teaspoon salt
¼ teaspoon pepper
4 tablespoons butter or margarine
parsley for garnish

Squeeze juice of one orange. Reserve 1 tablespoon and mix rest with Grand Marnier. Slice 2 oranges thinly and marinate for 1 hour in the orange juice and Grand Marnier. Salt and pepper fish and put in a broiling pan. Melt butter. Mix the reserved orange juice with half of the melted butter and pour over fish. Broil for 9 minutes or until done, basting frequently. When fish is done, remove to serving platter and surround fish with parsley and marinated oranges. Quickly mix rest of melted butter and orange marinade and pour over fish. Serves 4.

Pompano With a Twist

2 lbs. pompano
8 tablespoons butter or margarine, melted
¼ teaspoon onion salt
¼ teaspoon curry powder
1 teaspoon lemon peel, cut in thin strips
2 tablespoons dry white wine
2 tablespoons lemon juice
¼ teaspoon pepper

Lay fish on a shallow baking dish. Spoon 1 tablespoon of the butter over the fish and put in broiler. Combine all other ingredients and spoon over fish. Baste frequently. Broil for 10 minutes or until fish is done. Remove fish to serving platter and pour pan juices over fish. Serves 4.

Stewed to the Gills

Yachtman's Marlin

- 2 large slices marlin
- 3 tablespoons oil
- 1 clove garlic, mashed
- 3 green onions, chopped
- 1 teaspoon oregano
- 1 cup bread crumbs
- 2 tablespoons grated Parmesan cheese
- ¼ cup chopped parsley
- ⅓ cup water
- ⅓ cup sauterne

Roll the fish in the oil in the bottom of a baking pan. Sprinkle the fish with the garlic, chopped onions, oregano, and bread crumbs. Top with Parmesan cheese and parsley. Pour the water and wine around the fish and bake in a 400° oven for 45–60 minutes, until fish is done. Add more water if necessary. Serves 4.

Bouillabaisse With Wine—No. 1

- 3 lbs. boned fish cut in 3-inch squares—whiting, flounder, sole, haddock, perch, whitefish, red mullet or bass
- 8 shrimp, cooked and shelled
- ½ cup crab or lobster meat
- 1 dozen oysters, clams or mussels, in the shells
- 1 carrot, chopped
- 2 medium onions, chopped
- 2 leeks, chopped
- 1 clove garlic, minced
- ½ cup olive oil, 1 bay leaf
- 2 large tomatoes, quartered, or 1 cup canned tomatoes, strained
- 2 cups fish stock, clam juice or water
- ½ cup pimientos, minced
- ¼ teaspoon powdered saffron
- ⅓ cup Burgundy
- 1 teaspoon salt
- ½ teaspoon pepper
- juice of 1 lemon
- 8 slices toasted French bread
- 1 tablespoon chopped parsley

Cook carrots, leeks, onions and garlic in olive oil until golden brown. Add fish, tomatoes, bay leaf and stock. Simmer 20 minutes. Add shellfish, pimientos, saffron to taste, lemon juice and wine. Correct seasoning with salt and pepper. Put toast in deep dish. Add bouillabaisse and sprinkle with parsley. Serves 8.

Bouillabaisse No. 2

1 lb. shrimp or prawns, shelled
1 cracked crab
2 dozen clams, cleaned
1 lb. sea bass, cut into serving pieces
½ lb. bacon, fried and crumbled
1 6-oz. can tomato paste
1 8-oz. can tomato sauce
3 cups dry red wine
2 medium onions, chopped
1 4-oz. can mushrooms
2 teaspoons apple or cider vinegar
¾ teaspoon salt
¼ teaspoon pepper
1 bay leaf
¼ teaspoon each oregano, thyme, basel and powdered saffron
2 cloves garlic, minced

Mix last 11 ingredients in a large pot and simmer for 2 hours. Add fish, shellfish and bacon, and simmer for 30 minutes. Serve in individual bowls with plenty of French bread for dunking. Serves 6–8.

Stewed to the Gills

Another Round of Bouillabaisse

The day before:

1 beef bone	2 slices beef liver
1 veal knuckle	2–3 leeks
2 quarts water	4–5 stalks celery

Chop vegetables and cook all ingredients in a large soup kettle for 6 hours. Strain and cool. Add enough water to make 2 quarts. Or use canned bouillon to make 2 quarts of broth.

The day of serving:

7 lbs. fish (halibut or any other chowder fish), shrimp, clams, mussels, lobster and crab (cracked and cut into small pieces)	3 tablespoons oil
	½ cup flour
	1 small can okra
	3 cups canned tomatoes
	1 cup dry red wine
1 green pepper, chopped fine	1 can tomato soup
4 stalks celery, chopped fine	2 tablespoons caraway seeds
2 medium onions, chopped fine	1 teaspoon filé gumbo seasoning
2 large cloves garlic, chopped fine	salt
	pepper

Heat stock. Peel and clean shrimp and cook them in stock. Take shrimp out of stock and reserve shrimp for later. Cook green pepper, celery, onions and garlic in oil until light brown. Add flour and stir. Drain juice from okra and tomatoes and add juice and wine to bouillon. Add okra and tomatoes to onion and flour mixture. When this onion mixture is thick, add it to the boiling soup

stock. Add tomato soup, caraway seeds and filé gumbo seasoning to taste. Simmer as long as possible (a few hours). A half hour before serving, add fish, shellfish, and shrimp. Add salt and pepper to taste and thicken the soup with a little additional flour or arrowroot if necessary. Serves 10.

Smuggler's Fish

1½ cups leftover fish, flaked
6 large zucchini
½ cup bread crumbs
1 tablespoon dried parsley
1 tablespoon dry white wine

½ teaspoon oregano
3 tablespoons butter or margarine
3 tablespoons Parmesan cheese

Parboil zucchini for 5 minutes. Cut in half lengthwise and scoop out centers. Chop centers and add flaked fish, bread crumbs, wine, parsley and oregano. Mix and pile lightly into zucchini shells. Put in greased baking dish. Dot with butter and sprinkle with Parmesan cheese. Bake in a 350° oven for 20 minutes. Serve with Parsley Sauce. Serves 6.

Parsley Sauce

½ pint sour cream
juice of 1 lemon
1 large clove garlic, cut in quarters

½ teaspoon salt
1 bunch parsley, stems removed

Mix all ingredients in blender until smooth. Add more salt if necessary.

Stewed to the Gills

High Fish

1 cup leftover fish, flaked
1 can New England style clam chowder
¼ cup instant or granular flour
3 eggs, separated
1 teaspoon salt
dash white pepper
1 tablespoon sauterne
1 teaspoon paprika
1 teaspoon Worcestershire sauce

Preheat oven to 325°. Heat the chowder and, stirring constantly, add the flour. When the mixture is bubbling and thickened, stir in the fish and cook for another few minutes. Reduce the heat and add a few spoons of the mixture to the well-beaten egg yolks, then pour the egg mixture back into the pan and cook for another 2 minutes. Add all the other ingredients, with the exception of the egg whites, and cook another 2 minutes, stirring constantly. Remove from fire and let cool. Do not allow mixture to get cold. Beat egg whites very stiff and fold into the fish mixture. Pour into an ungreased 7-inch soufflé dish and bake 30 minutes. Serve immediately with SAUTÉED CUCUMBER BALLS. Serves 4.

Sautéed Cucumber Balls

4 cucumbers
6 tablespoons butter
dash salt
dash pepper
lemon juice

Peel cucumbers. With a melon ball cutter, make as many balls as possible. Heat butter very hot in a skillet and sauté the cucumbers for 15 minutes, turning them over occasionally. Sprinkle with salt and pepper and finish with a few squirts of lemon juice. Serves 4.

Mellow Fish

- 6 pieces fish such as sole, poached and cooled
- 2 tablespoons unflavored gelatin
- 1 bottle clam juice
- 1 cup dry white wine
- ½ teaspoon Dijon mustard
- 1½ teaspoons salt
- 1½ teaspoons sugar
- dash cayenne pepper
- 1 cup chopped celery
- ½ cup chopped pimientos
- salad greens

Dissolve gelatin in clam juice and heat for 30 seconds stirring constantly. Remove from fire and add wine, mustard, salt, sugar and cayenne. Chill for 20–30 minutes, stirring the mixture occasionally. When thick, add celery, pimientos and fish cut into pieces about 1 inch square. Pour into oiled mold and chill at least 4 hours. Unmold on greens and serve with Mellow Sauce. Serves 6.

Mellow Sauce

- ½ cup mayonnaise
- ½ cup sour cream
- 1 small cucumber, chopped
- 1 teaspoon capers
- 1 teaspoon lemon juice

Combine all ingredients and chill for an hour before serving.

Soup Toddy

1½ cups cold flaked fish
1 can cream of potato soup
1 can cream of celery soup
1 soup can half and half
2 tablespoons dry sherry

Combine all ingredients in a large pan. Heat slowly (do not allow to boil). Taste for seasoning. If necessary, add salt and pepper. Serve hot with chowder biscuits. Serves 4.

Pub Kippers

4 kippers
4 tablespoons sweet butter
1 teaspoon dry white wine
1 teaspoon lemon juice
½ tablespoon dried parsley
½ teaspoon sweet basil

Soften and cream butter. Add wine, lemon juice, parsley and sweet basil. Reshape butter into oblong form. Refrigerate for at least 30 minutes. Broil kippers until done. Put on serving platter and place ¼ of the herb butter on each kipper. Serves 4.

Morning-After Eggs

⅛ lb. smoked sturgeon or smoked whitefish, flaked
6 tablespoons butter
2 tablespoons flour
1½ cups half and half
1 tablespoon lemon juice
4 tablespoons dry white wine
8 eggs
dash salt
dash white pepper

Make cream sauce first. Melt 2 tablespoons butter in a saucepan over low heat. Stir in flour and mix until smooth. Slowly add half and half, stirring constantly until sauce thickens. Add 2 tablespoons wine, lemon juice and fish. Keep warm while omelet is cooking. Beat eggs, 2 tablespoons wine, salt and pepper until light and fluffy. Melt remaining butter over low heat in large omelet pan or skillet. Pour in eggs and cook slowly until set. Slip onto serving platter. If you're not an experienced omelet maker and want a fail-proof method, cook omelet until almost set. Put under hot broiler for about 20–30 seconds to set top. Then slip onto serving platter. Pour 2/3 of the sauce over half of the omelet. Fold omelet in half to cover sauce. Pour rest of sauce over omelet. Serves 4.

Soupe Superieur

4 teaspoons red caviar
1 tablespoon unflavored gelatin
1 can beef consommé
1 soup can vegetable juice, such as V8

1 tablespoon dry white wine
4 tablespoons sour cream

Dissolve gelatin in ½ can beef consommé. Heat rest of consommé, vegetable juice, and wine. Stir in gelatin mixture. Refrigerate until jelled. Spoon into small serving dishes such as sherbet glasses. Put a tablespoon of sour cream on soup. Put 1 teaspoon caviar in the center of the sour cream. Serves 4.

Caviar Sauterne en Gelée

6 oz. red caviar
1 envelope unflavored gelatin
2 cans consommé madrilene
¼ cup chopped onion
⅛ cup finely chopped parsley
3 tablespoons lemon juice
2 tablespoons sauterne
½ pint sour cream
1 teaspoon dill weed

Soften the gelatin in ¼ cup consommé. Heat remaining consommé and add gelatin mixture. Add wine, lemon juice, parsley and onion. Stir well and pour into a lightly oiled, deep, 3-cup mold. Set until firm. With a small spoon carefully scoop out enough aspic to leave a shell in the bowl. Put the extra aspic in a small pan. Lift the caviar from its juices with a fork and place in the cavity made by scooping out the aspic. Melt the extra aspic and pour over the caviar. Refrigerate to set again. Unmold. Pass a bowl of sour cream that has been blended with the dill weed. Thinly sliced rye bread make a good accompaniment. Serves 6–8.

Toasts

6 flat anchovy fillets
4 slices white bread, toasted
6 tablespoons butter
½ teaspoon paprika
1 tablespoon Worcestershire sauce
2 tablespoons tomato paste
½ teaspoon salt
1 teaspoon lemon juice
1 teaspoon dry vermouth
2 tablespoons chopped parsley
1 hard-boiled egg, chopped

Mash fillets with a fork. Thoroughly beat all the ingredients except parsley and hard-boiled egg. Add anchovies. Spread on the toast. Cut each slice in three strips. Garnish with chopped egg and parsley. An appetizer sufficient for 4–6.

Drinker's Cheese

3 oz. caviar
1 envelope unflavored gelatin
¼ cup warm water
1 8-oz. package Neufchatel cheese
¼ cup mayonnaise
¼ cup sour cream
1½ teaspoons paprika
1 teaspoon salt
¼ teaspoon white pepper
½ teaspoon garlic salt
¼ teaspoon onion powder
¼ teaspoon dill weed
1 tablespoon lemon juice
1 tablespoon vodka

Dissolve gelatin in warm water. In a large bowl beat the cheese until very smooth and gradually add the mayonnaise, sour cream, paprika, salt, pepper, garlic salt and onion powder. Beat well until smooth and creamy. Fold in caviar and dill weed. Add the lemon and vodka to the gelatin mixture. Combine with cheese mixture. Stir well. Taste for seasoning. Must be very tangy. Add more lemon juice if necessary. Oil a small (2 cup), very fancy mold and pour in the mixture. Chill overnight. Carefully unmold on a serving plate. Serve with very simple crisp crackers as an accompaniment to drinks. Serves 6.

CHAPTER FIVE

Tuna Ties One On

1 7-oz. can tuna, flaked
7 large black olives, sliced
1 small onion, grated
1 teaspoon salt
¼ teaspoon powdered thyme
⅛ teaspoon allspice
⅛ teaspoon curry powder
dash of pepper
1 teaspoon prepared mustard
⅓ cup butter or margarine
⅓ cup flour
2 cups milk
2 tablespoons dry sherry
3 hard-boiled eggs cut in eighths
3 eggs, separated
4 slices of toast, cut into ½-inch cubes

Here's one soufflé that works every time. You don't need to have the right vibrations or know any incantations to get it to rise and stay up. Mix the olives, tuna, grated onion and all the seasonings. Melt the butter in a saucepan over low heat. Blend in the flour slowly and mix to a smooth consistency. Slowly stir in milk; continue stirring until sauce is thick and shiny (about 15 or 20 minutes). Add sherry. Remove the sauce from the heat and pour half of it into the tuna mixture. Place in a 2-quart greased baking dish. Put the hard-boiled eggs on top. Mix the 3 egg yolks and add to the remaining white sauce. Cook over low heat, stirring constantly, for 3 minutes. Remove from heat and set aside to cool. Beat the egg whites until they form peaks. Fold into the sauce. Fold in the toast cubes and carefully spoon over the tuna. Bake in a 375° oven for 35 minutes until the top is golden brown. Be patient and don't look! Serve immediately. Serves 4.

Falstaff's Tuna

1 7-oz. can tuna
2 packages frozen spinach soufflé
½ cup sour cream

½ cup mayonnaise
2 tablespoons dry sherry
¼ teaspoon nutmeg

Bake spinach soufflé according to directions on package. While soufflé is cooking, mix sour cream, mayonnaise, sherry and nutmeg. Put sauce into a small pyrex bowl or cup. Set in a pan of simmering water to heat. Drain and flake tuna. Add to sauce and mix thoroughly. Keep warm until soufflé is done. Transfer soufflé to serving dish. Spoon sauce over soufflé. Serves 4.

Here's Tuna

1 large can tuna, drained and flaked
1 can cream of celery soup
⅓ cup dry white wine
2 jars marinated artichokes

3 cups cooked rice
¼ cup bread crumbs
2 tablespoons butter or margarine

Mix celery soup, wine, and marinade from one of the jars of artichokes. In a greased casserole layer quartered artichokes, tuna, rice and sauce, ending with sauce. Sprinkle top with bread crumbs and dot with butter. Bake in a 350° oven for 30 minutes. Serves 4.

Wine Seller's Tuna

1 7-oz. can chunk style tuna
1 cup cooked rice
½ small onion, grated
½ teaspoon dried parsley
1 teaspoon curry powder

1 can cream of mushroom soup
2 tablespoons dry sherry
2 hard-boiled eggs, quartered
dash of paprika

Mix the rice, undrained tuna, onion, parsley, curry and ½ can mushroom soup. Add sherry. Gently fold in the hard-boiled eggs. Put the mixture in a greased casserole. Spread remaining mushroom soup over top. Sprinkle with paprika. Bake in a 400° oven for 20 minutes. Serves 4.

Schooner Tuna

1 7-oz. can tuna, flaked
½ lb. fresh mushrooms, sliced
2 tablespoons butter or margarine
1 6-oz. package fine noodles, cooked and drained
1 cup cooked green peas
½ cup green or ripe olives, sliced
2 tablespoons butter or margarine

2 tablespoons flour
2 cups milk or light cream
2 tablespoons flat beer
1 cup shredded cheddar cheese
¼ cup bread crumbs
1 tablespoon butter or margarine

Sauté mushrooms in 2 tablespoons butter until tender (about 5 minutes). Arrange hot noodles in a buttered 1½ quart casserole. Cover with mushrooms, layer of peas, olives and tuna. Melt 2 tablespoons butter in saucepan. Add flour and stir until smooth. Slowly add milk, stirring until hot and of medium white sauce consistency. Add flat beer. Melt cheese in the sauce and pour over the casserole. Mix bread crumbs and remaining butter and sprinkle on top of mixture. Bake in a 350° oven for 30 minutes or until browned. Serves 4.

Clubhouse Tuna

12½ oz. chunk style tuna
1 lb. package macaroni
1 pint sour cream
2 tablespoons dry sherry
½ lb. Tillamook cheese, grated
salt
pepper

Cook macaroni according to directions on package. Drain, but do not rinse. Mix with sour cream, sherry, salt and pepper to taste. Flake tuna. Layer macaroni, cheese and tuna in a greased casserole, ending with grated cheese. Bake uncovered in a 350° oven for 20 minutes. Serves 6.

Tuna on a Toot

1 7-oz. can tuna, drained and flaked
1 3-oz. package cream cheese
1 can cream of mushroom soup
2 tablespoons dry sherry
1½ tablespoons pimiento
1 tablespoon prepared mustard
1 tablespoon chopped onion
¼ cup milk
6 oz. macaroni, cooked and drained
½ cup bread crumbs
2 tablespoons butter or margarine

Soften cream cheese and blend in soup and sherry, using an electric or hand beater. Stir in tuna, pimiento, mustard, onion, milk and macaroni. Grease a 2-quart casserole and spoon tuna mixture into casserole carefully. Sprinkle top with crumbs and dot with butter. Bake in a 375° oven for 25 minutes. Serves 4.

Smashed Tuna

1 7-oz. can solid pack
   whitemeat tuna
1 cup mayonnaise
¼ cup lemon juice
¼ cup dry white wine

2 cloves garlic, mashed
1 tablespoon anchovy
   paste
2 tablespoons capers

Drain tuna. Put in a small bowl and mash thoroughly. Mix all other ingredients and add to tuna, blending completely. Cover and chill. This is a simple version of the Italian sauce, Vitello Tonnato. It adds zest to cold veal, fish, turkey, chicken and other cold meats.

Tipsy Tuna

2½ lbs. fresh tuna, sliced
1 cup oil
2 large onions, sliced
3 cloves garlic
1 cup vinegar
¼ cup dry white wine

2 bay leaves
2 teaspoons whole black
   peppercorns
1 teaspoon salt
2–3 small pieces dried red
   pepper

Salt tuna and fry in the oil until lightly browned. Place the fish in a crockery or earthenware casserole. Fry onion and garlic in oil about 5 minutes. Add vinegar, wine, bay leaves and black and red pepper. Bring to a boil and pour over fish. If the fish is not covered, add more vinegar. Cover and marinate for at least 2 days. The fish keeps for several weeks in the refrigerator—and may be eaten as an hors d'oeuvre or served as a first course.

CHAPTER SIX

Oak Barrel Shrimp

1½ lbs. shrimp
3 tablespoons dry white wine
1 large clove garlic, minced
6 tablespoons soft butter or margarine
juice of 1 lemon

Preheat oven to 550°. Split shrimp, still in shells, and arrange in a shallow dish or broiler. Drizzle wine on shrimp. Mix garlic and butter and spread on split shrimp. Broil until shells are charred and meat is pink. Remove from broiler and sprinkle liberally with lemon juice. Serves 4.

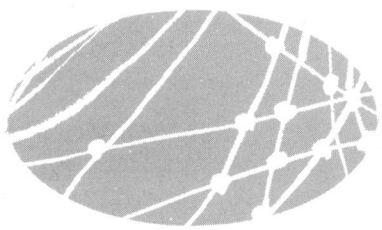

Shrimp Cheerio

1½ lbs. shrimp, shelled
1 cup mayonnaise
juice of ½ lemon
4 tablespoons dry white wine
¼ teaspoon curry powder

Put shrimp in shallow pan. Thin mayonnaise with the lemon and wine. Add curry powder to taste. Coat shrimp with mayonnaise and broil 3 minutes on each side or until shrimp is pink and mayonnaise is brown and bubbly. Serves 4.

Soused, Sauced, Smashed ...

Saloon Shrimp

2 lbs. raw shrimp, shelled
2 green peppers, cut in eighths
2 medium onions, cut in eighths
12 cherry tomatoes
3 tablespoons prepared barbecue sauce
1 8-oz. can tomato sauce
1 tablespoon lemon juice
1 tablespoon dry white wine

Alternate the peppers, onions, tomatoes and shrimp on skewers. Lay the skewers on a tray. Mix barbecue sauce, tomato sauce, lemon juice and wine. With a pastry brush, coat both sides of each skewer with the sauce. Let stand for about an hour. Barbecue skewers or cook in broiler about 3 minutes on each side or until shrimp are done. Serves 6.

Soaked Shrimp

2 lbs. shrimp, cooked and shelled
1 cup dry sherry
1 tablespoon lemon juice
¼ teaspoon black pepper
1 teaspoon dried basil
1 clove garlic, mashed
¼ cup oil
½ cup butter or margarine, melted

Combine all ingredients except shrimp and butter. Marinate the shrimp in the sauce for 2 hours. Line broiler pan with aluminum foil and heat for 10 minutes. Lift shrimp from marinade. Heat the marinade and add the melted butter. Arrange shrimp in broiler pan and pour sauce over shrimp, coating them well. Broil 3 inches from flame. Turn as soon as shrimp are pink and broil other side. Do not overcook. Serve with sauce left in pan. Serves 6.

Shrimp Côte de Provence

2 lbs. shrimp, shelled
¼ cup butter or margarine
¼ cup oil
½ teaspoon salt
dash fresh ground pepper
2 large cloves garlic, minced
½ cup chopped fresh parsley or 2 tablespoons dried parsley
2 tablespoons vin rosé

Heat the oil and butter in a frying pan. Add the shrimp and cook quickly for about 4 minutes until shrimp is almost done. Stir occasionally. Add the salt, pepper, garlic, parsley and wine. Stir and cook for 1 minute longer. Serve shrimp with all of the sauce poured over them. Serves 6.

Shrimp Vino

2 lbs. shrimp, cooked and shelled
½ lb. mushrooms, sliced
6 green onions, chopped
1 cup bottled Italian dressing
½ cup dry white wine
1 cup bread crumbs
6 tablespoons grated Parmesan cheese
4 tablespoons dried parsley
8 tablespoons butter or margarine

One hour before cooking, marinate shrimp, mushrooms and green onions in Italian dressing and white wine. When ready to cook, spread all in a shallow casserole. Sprinkle with parsley, bread crumbs and cheese. Dot with butter. Bake in a 400° oven for 10 minutes. Serves 6.

Soused, Sauced, Smashed...

Singapore Sling Shrimp

2 lbs. shrimp, cooked and shelled (save cooking water)
½ small onion, finely chopped
1 tablespoon butter or margarine
2 tablespoons curry powder
1 oz. preserved ginger, sliced
½ teaspoon powdered ginger
½ teaspoon chili powder
1 bouillon cube
½ cup boiling water
1 cucumber, diced
1 tablespoon lemon juice
2 tablespoons light rum
pinch cayenne

Sauté chopped onion in butter until onion is golden. Add curry, preserved ginger, powdered ginger, chiil powder and bouillon cube (which has been dissolved in the boiling water). Mix and simmer for 15 minutes, stirring occasionally. Add shrimp, cucumber, lemon juice, rum, cayenne and 1 cup of the water in which you have cooked the shrimp. Simmer until vegetables are tender. Serve with rice and chutney. Serves 6.

Shrimp Sling

1½ lbs. shrimp, cooked and shelled
1 can frozen shrimp soup
1 medium onion, finely chopped
2 tablespoons butter or margarine
½ pint sour cream at room temperature
1 teaspoon curry powder
2 tablespoons dry sherry

Sauté onion in butter until transparent. Add frozen soup. Cook over low heat, stirring frequently, until soup has dissolved and is smooth. Add sour cream, curry and sherry. Mix and simmer for 10 minutes. Add shrimp and cook for an additional 5 minutes. Serve with rice and curry boys: chopped peanuts, shredded coconut, chopped parsley, chopped green pepper, chopped green onions, tomato wedges, sliced bananas, chutney, etc. Serves 4.

Sherried Shrimp and Deviled Eggs

1 lb. shrimp, cooked and shelled
6 hard-boiled eggs
1 teaspoon Worcestershire sauce
1 tablespoon mayonnaise
¼ teaspoon dry mustard
dash salt
dash pepper
½ lb. fresh mushrooms, sliced
2 tablespoons butter or margarine

Sauce

4 tablespoons butter or margarine
4 tablespoons flour
2 cups milk
½ teaspoon salt
1 tablespoon dry sherry
2 tablespoons mayonnaise
½ teaspoon dry mustard
1 cup grated American cheese

Start this casserole by preparing deviled eggs. Cut the hard-boiled eggs in half lengthwise and scoop out the yolks into a mixing bowl. Mash and add Worcestershire sauce, mayonnaise, mustard, salt and pepper. Mix and stuff yolks back into the egg whites. Put the deviled eggs in a single layer in a casserole. Sauté the mushrooms in butter. Place mushrooms and shrimp around eggs. Make the sauce by melting butter in a saucepan. Add the flour and stir until smooth and thick. Add milk slowly, stirring constantly, and heat until sauce thickens. Add the cheese, mustard, salt, sherry and mayonnaise. Continue stirring until the sauce thickens. Pour the sauce over the shrimp and eggs and bake in a 350° oven for 20 minutes. Serves 4.

Wined Shrimp de Jonghe

2 lbs. shrimp, shelled
¼ cup butter or margarine
1⅓ cups hot milk
1 cup bread crumbs
½ cup minced fresh parsley or 3 tablespoons dried parsley
1 small clove garlic, minced
1½ teaspoons salt
⅛ teaspoon pepper
½ cup soft butter or margarine
1 tablespoon dry white wine
4 tablespoons grated Parmesan cheese
¼ cup melted butter or margarine

Split shrimp in half lengthwise and sauté in ¼ cup butter. Put in a baking dish or casserole. Pour hot milk over crumbs and mix well. Let stand until thick. If mixture is too thick, add a little more milk. Add parsley, garlic, salt, pepper, wine and ½ cup soft butter. Mix and spread over shrimp. Sprinkle with cheese and drizzle melted cheese. Bake in a 350° oven for 30 minutes. Serves 6–8.

Soused Shrimp and Asparagus

2 lbs. shrimp, cooked and shelled
2 packages frozen asparagus spears or 1½ lbs. fresh asparagus
4 tablespoons butter or margarine
4 tablespoons flour
1½ cups milk
2 tablespoons dry sherry
½ cup grated Parmesan cheese
1 egg yolk, slightly beaten
½ cup heavy cream
1 teaspoon salt
dash pepper, cayenne, nutmeg
dash paprika

Cook asparagus. Drain well on paper towels and arrange in a shallow baking dish. Melt butter in a sauce pan and add flour. Stir until smooth. Stir in the milk gradually. Add sherry. Cook until thick. Add the cheese (reserve a little for topping) and mix well. Combine cream with egg yolk. Add slowly to sauce, stirring constantly. Add salt, pepper, cayenne and nutmeg. Continue stirring over low heat for 2–3 minutes. Add shrimp and mix. Pour sauce and shrimp over asparagus. Sprinkle with paprika and remaining cheese. Put pan under broiler for 3 minutes to brown slightly. Serves 6.

Winelover's Jambalaya

2 lbs. shrimp, shelled
1 quart clam juice
1 quart dry white wine
2 medium onions, minced
½ cup diced salt pork
2 cups brown rice
2 tomatoes, peeled and minced
½ bay leaf
½ lb. fresh lean pork, cubed
½ lb. smoked ham, cubed
½ lb. mushrooms, sliced
½ cup Madeira wine
¼ cup Burgundy
salt
pepper

Bring clam juice and white wine to boil in a large pot. Add shrimp, reduce heat and simmer until shrimp turn pink. Remove from heat and cool shrimp in broth. When cool, remove shrimp from broth and reserve both shrimp and broth. In a large skillet or flameproof casserole sauté onions and salt pork over high heat until golden brown. Add rice and cook, stirring for 1 minute. Add tomatoes, bay leaf, pork, smoked ham and mushrooms. Remove fatty pieces of salt pork and discard. Cover with 5 cups reserved broth, Madeira and Burgundy. Bring to boil over high heat. Reduce heat to low and cook covered for 30 minutes. Add reserved shrimp. Cook for 10 minutes more. All the liquid should be absorbed. Correct seasoning with salt and pepper if necessary. Serves 8.

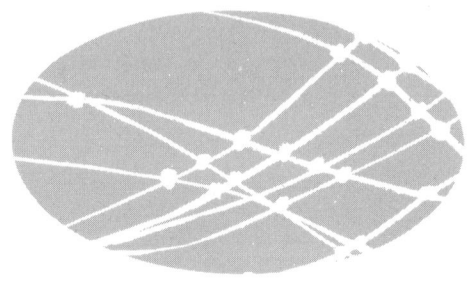

Alehouse Shrimp

1½ lbs. cooked medium-size shrimp
8 oz. wide egg noodles
1 teaspoon salt
6 tablespoons butter or margarine
4 eggs
1 can Vichyssoise
½ cup ale

Cook noodles al dente. Drain well. Place half in a greased oven-to-table open dish. Dot with half of the butter. Cover the noodles with the shrimp and sprinkle with salt. Put rest of noodles over the shrimp and dot with the remaining butter. Beat eggs thoroughly with an electric beater, and then beat in the soup. When well blended stir in the ale. Pour over the noodle-shrimp mixture. Bake in a 375° oven for 25 minutes. Serves 4.

Paella Manzanillo

- 2 lbs. shrimp, cooked and shelled
- 6 small chicken breasts, halved
- ½ teaspoon salt
- ¼ teaspoon pepper
- 3 tablespoons oil
- 4 tablespoons butter or margarine
- 2 tablespoons chicken stock base
- 1 cup water
- 2 12-oz. cans clam juice
- ½ teaspoon powdered saffron
- ½ cup Manzanillo sherry
- 1 8-oz. can clams
- 3 cups rice
- 2 medium onions, chopped
- 2 cloves garlic, minced
- ¼ cup chopped parsley
- 1 cup chopped celery, including leaves
- 3 tablespoons oil
- 4 tablespoons butter or margarine
- ½ lb. chorizo sausage, cut in 1-inch pieces (optional)
- 1 small can sliced pimiento
- ½ teaspoon rosemary
- ½ teaspoon sweet basil
- ½ cup walnuts, coarsely chopped

Paella is the Spanish version of "getting it all together." Find your largest shallow pot—a turkey roaster will do. Season chicken with salt and pepper. Sauté in 3 tablespoons oil and 4 tablespoons butter in a skillet until almost done. While chicken is cooking, dissolve chicken stock base in water. Add clam juice, saffron, sherry, the liquid from the can of clams, and enough water to make 6 cups liquid. Put liquid in a saucepan and bring to a boil. Add rice and cover. Turn fire down low. Steam rice for 25 minutes. While rice is cooking, sauté onions, garlic, parsley, and celery in rest of oil and butter until onions are golden. Remove vegetables to roaster and in same pan quickly fry the chorizo. Add chicken, shrimp, rice, clams chorizo, pimiento, rosemary, sweet basil, and walnuts to roaster. Mix gently and correct seasoning with salt and pepper. Cover with a lid or foil and heat in a 325° oven for 20–30 minutes or until hot. Serves 12.

Soused, Sauced, Smashed . . .

Sazerac Shrimp Creole

- 2 lbs. shrimp, cooked and shelled
- 1 medium onion, finely chopped
- 1 small green pepper, finely chopped
- 2 tablespoons butter or margarine
- 2 tablespoons flour
- 1 bay leaf, crushed
- ¼ cup diced celery
- 1 teaspoon parsley
- dash cayenne
- ¼ teaspoon Tabasco
- ½ teaspoon salt
- 1 6-oz. can tomato paste
- 2 tablespoons light rum
- dash Angostura bitters
- 2 cups water

Sauté onion and green pepper in butter until onion is yellow. Blend in flour and mix until smooth. Add all the other ingredients except shrimp. Cook slowly, stirring occasionally, until thickened. This takes about 30 minutes. Add the shrimp and continue cooking a few minutes until shrimp are heated. Serve with rice. Serves 6.

Shrimp Salut!

- 2 lbs. shrimp, shelled
- 1 cup canned tomatoes, drained
- 1 teaspoon mixed Italian seasoning
- 1 8-oz. can tomato sauce
- 1 clove garlic, minced
- juice of ½ lemon
- ½ teaspoon sugar
- ¼ cup dry white wine

Mix all ingredients except shrimp and bring to a boil. Turn heat to medium flame and add shrimp. Cook for 4–5 minutes until shrimp is done. Do not overcook shrimp. Serves 6.

Shrimp Swizzle

- 2 lbs. shrimp, cooked and shelled
- 2 large onions, coarsely diced
- 1 clove garlic, crushed
- 1 bay leaf
- 2 tablespoons oil
- 2 tablespoons butter or margarine
- ½ teaspoon salt
- ¼ teaspoon coarse ground pepper
- 3 cups canned whole tomatoes
- 1 small can chunk pineapple
- 3 tablespoons dry sherry
- ½ teaspoon MSG or Accent

Sauté the onions, garlic and bay leaf in oil and butter until the onions are golden brown. Salt and pepper lightly. Add the tomatoes, reserving the juice. Break up tomatoes gently. Simmer for 15 minutes. Add 3 tablespoons of the liquid from the canned tomatoes, 3 tablespoons of the pineapple juice, sherry and MSG. Add pineapple and shrimp to sauce and mix well. Correct the seasoning and simmer until the shrimp and pineapple are heated. Serves 6.

Shrimp Mirin

- ¼ lb. tiny cooked shrimp
- 6 green onions, chopped
- 3 tablespoons butter or margarine
- 2 cans bean sprouts, drained
- 1 tablespoon soy sauce
- 1 tablespoon mirin or dry sherry
- 1 tablespoon chopped parsley

Sauté green onions in butter for 3 minutes. Stir in bean sprouts and shrimp. Heat thoroughly. Add soy sauce and wine. Mix well and sprinkle with chopped parsley. Serve as a side dish. Serves 4.

Saki Shrimp Ami and Kai

1 lb. shrimp, cooked and shelled
1 can frozen shrimp soup, defrosted
½ teaspoon soy sauce
1 tablespoon saki or dry sherry
3 hard-boiled eggs, sliced
1 5-oz. can water chestnuts, drained and sliced

Heat soup, shrimp, soy sauce and wine together in a saucepan, stirring frequently. Carefully add egg slices and water chestnuts. Heat for a few minutes and serve with rice. Serves 4.

Perfect Shrimp Subgum

1 lb. shrimp, cooked, shelled and cooled
1 package frozen string beans
2 tablespoons cornstarch
2 tablespoons soy sauce
1 teaspoon MSG or Accent
2 tablespoons bourbon
¼ cup cold water
2 chicken bouillon cubes
1½ cups hot water
4 tablespoons peanut oil
½ teaspoon salt
⅛ teaspoon pepper
½ teaspoon powdered ginger
2 cloves garlic, crushed
2 cups celery, sliced diagonally
1 can bean sprouts, drained
1 small can water chestnuts
3 green onions, sliced
3 tablespoons sliced toasted almonds

Cook the frozen string beans and drain. Mix the cornstarch, soy sauce, MSG, bourbon and water. Dissolve the bouillon cubes in hot water. In a hot skillet, put the oil, salt, pepper, ginger and garlic. Mix and add the bouillon and all the vegetables except the green onions and green beans. Mix well and cover. Turn the flame down and cook for 10 minutes. Add the shrimp, string beans and green ions. Mix and stir for 2 minutes. Add the cornstarch mixture and stir until the sauce thickens and is glossy (about 6 minutes). Pour into a serving bowl, top with the almonds and serve immediately. Fried or white rice and Chinese fried noodles complete the meal. Serves 4.

Neat Shrimp Newburg

2 lbs. shrimp, cooked and shelled
1 cup canned white sauce
½ cup dry sherry
1 teaspoon onion powder
1 teaspoon garlic salt
paprika

In the top of a double boiler, mix the white sauce, sherry, onion powder and garlic salt. Add enough paprika to turn the sauce pink. When sauce is hot, add shrimp. Continue heating until shrimp are hot. Serve with rice. Serves 6.

Sauced Shrimp

2 lbs. shrimp, shelled and split lengthwise
4 tablespoons butter or margarine
4 tablespoons minced onions
½ cup dry white wine
1 pint sour cream
2 teaspoons dried parsley
1 teaspoon dill weed
1 teaspoon salt

Sauté the shrimp and onion in butter until shrimp are pink and tender (about 5 minutes). Mix wine and sour cream until smooth; stir in parsley, dill and salt, and add to shrimp. Mix very carefully and continue cooking until sauce is hot, stirring frequently. Serve with rice. Serves 6.

Soused, Sauced, Smashed . . .

Tosspot's Tart

¼ lb. cooked small shrimp
1 package refrigerated unbaked crescent rolls
6 slices bacon, diced
1 medium onion. chopped
¼ medium green pepper, chopped
1 small stalk celery, chopped
¼ cup flour
¼ teaspoon salt
1 8-oz. can small whole clams
1 tablespoon dry vermouth
2 eggs, beaten
1 2-oz. can chopped mushrooms, including liquid
½ pint sour cream
paprika

Make a bottom crust by unfolding crescent rolls and laying them so they overlap in a greased 10-inch pie pan. Press together so dough is smooth. Fry bacon until almost done. Add onion, green pepper and celery and cook until onion is transparent. Stir in flour and salt. Add clams, including liquid, and vermouth. Stir constantly until thick. Stir a little of the hot sauce into the egg until mixed thoroughly and return to clam mixture. Add shrimp and mushrooms and stir for a few seconds. Spoon filling into pie crust. Carefully spread sour cream over filling. Sprinkle with paprika and bake in a 350° oven for 30 minutes. Serves 6.

Shrimp Calvados

1 cup small cooked shrimp
¼ cup finely chopped onion
3 tablespoons butter
2 envelopes unflavored gelatin
1½ cups ginger beer
1 teaspoon curry
½ cup brown sugar
3 tablespoons cider vinegar
3 tablespoons calvados
4 cups yogurt
paprika
salad greens

In a large skillet sauté onions in butter until limp. Combine the gelatin with the ginger beer. Stir until well dissolved. Add curry, brown sugar, cider vinegar and calvados to the gelatin and stir well. Pour into the skillet and heat on a low flame for 10 minutes stirring constantly. Remove from heat. Pour mixture into a deep bowl. With a rotary beater start beating slowly, and gradually beat in the yogurt. Beat until mixture is smooth and creamy. Pour into a 5–6 cup yogurt ring mold and chill until firm. Unmold on greens and fill center with shrimp sprinkled lightly with paprika. Serve as a salad, buffet or main course. Serves 4.

Bloody Mary Shrimp

½ lb. small cooked shrimp
2 cups highly spiced tomato
　juice cocktail
1 tablespoon vodka

1 package lemon flavored
　gelatin
dash of Tabasco sauce
2 bunches watercress

Heat 1 cup juice and dissolve gelatin in it. Add the remaining juice, Tabasco and vodka. Stir thoroughly. Place in refrigerator to chill until thick, but not set. Oil a small, high bowl or mold (2–2½ cup capacity) and then wipe well with a paper towel. Stir shrimp into thickened aspic. Pour into mold and chill until set. Clean and dry the watercress and arrange a layer of it on a medium-size serving plate. Unmold the shrimp in the center. Serves 4 as a first course. Pass the sauce separately.

Cucumber Sauce

2 cucumbers
1 teaspoon salt
½ cup vinegar

3 green onions, chopped very fine
½ cup sour cream

Peel and slice the cucumbers very thin. Sprinkle with salt. Let stand for 1 hour. Squeeze out all the liquid and combine cucumbers with vinegar, green onions and sour cream.

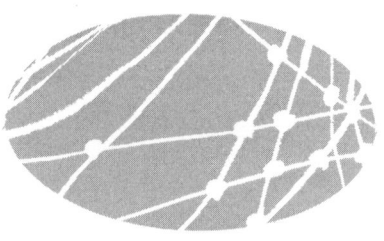

Old Soak Shrimp

½ lb. small cooked shrimp
½ lb. fresh mushrooms
1 can pitted ripe olives, drained
1½ cups bottled oil and vinegar dressing

½ cup dry white wine
2 tablespoons chopped parsley
1 jar marinated artichoke hearts, drained

Wash, stem and dry mushrooms and slice very thin. Slice the olives. Combine mushrooms, olives and shrimp in a bowl and pour the dressing and wine over them. Refrigerate for 3 hours. Serve in salad bowls as a first course. Lift the salad from the dressing into the bowls and decorate with artichoke hearts and a sprinkle of parsley. Serves 4.

Shrimp Margarita

½ lb. small cooked shrimp
lettuce
1 tablespoon tequila
1 avocado
1 onion, minced
½ cup sour cream
1 teaspoon lime juice
chili powder to taste
1 cup crisp corn chips

Line a small salad bowl with torn lettuce. Place shrimp on lettuce. Mash avocado with a fork and combine with sour cream, tequila, lime juice and onion. Stir well and add chili powder to taste. Pour over shrimp. Crumble the corn chips and scatter over the salad. Serves 4.

High Living Shrimp

2 lbs. shrimp, cooked, shelled and chilled
salad greens
4 zucchini, cut in ½-inch slices
1 cauliflower, cut in chunks or flowers
1 basket cherry tomatoes
1 large avocado, cut in thick slices or pieces

Place salad greens in a salad bowl. Skewer shrimp, zucchini, cauliflower, tomatoes and avocado on small skewers, such as Japanese bamboo skewers. Repeat as space will allow. Put any remaining vegetables or shrimp in salad bowl. Stand the skewers upright in the salad greens. Serve salad and pass dressing separately. Serves 6.

Soused, Sauced, Smashed . . .

Creamy Wine Dressing

1 cup mayonnaise
½ cup oil
¼ cup lemon juice
2 tablespoons dry sherry
¼ cup chili sauce
2 tablespoons green olives, chopped

1 teaspoon horseradish
1 teaspoon Worcestershire sauce
¼ teaspoon salt

Beat mayonnaise until light and fluffy. Add oil, lemon juice and sherry and mix again. Add other ingredients and mix. Add more salt if necessary.

Soup on the Rocks

1 can frozen cream of shrimp soup
1 soup can light cream or half and half

¼ teaspoon curry powder
2 tablespoons dry sherry
12 tiny cooked shrimp

Defrost shrimp soup according to directions on can. Add cream and heat gently. Add curry to taste and mix thoroughly. Stir in sherry. Chill at least 6 hours. Serve in small soup bowls or seafood icers. Top with tiny shrimp. Serves 4.

Spiked Shrimp Hors d'Oeuvres

2 lbs. shrimp, cooked and shelled
1 medium onion, sliced thin
1 clove garlic, minced
1 lemon, sliced thin
2 cups oil
1 cup vinegar
2 tablespoons dry white wine
1 teaspoon salt
½ teaspoon freshly ground pepper
1 teaspoon dried salad herbs
1 teaspoon dried parsley

Mix the dressing (oil, vinegar, wine, salt, pepper, salad herbs, and dried parsley). Pour dressing over the shrimp, onions, garlis and lemon. Cover and marinate overnight, mixing occasionally. To serve, drain off dressing. Arrange lemon slices on top. Serve with picks. Serves 12.

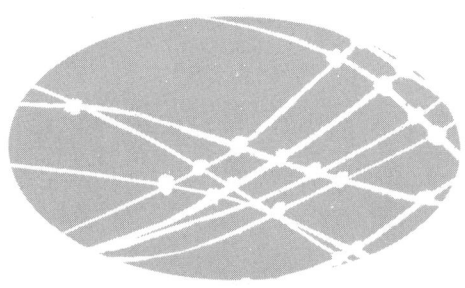

Soused, Sauced, Smashed . . .

CHAPTER SEVEN

CROCKED CRAB

Winemaster's Cioppino

2 cracked crabs
1 cup oil
1 large onion, chopped
1 cup parsley, chopped
½ lb. mushrooms, sliced
1 teaspoon salt
½ teaspoon pepper
9 cups canned tomatoes
3 8-oz. cans tomato sauce
⅓ cup dry red wine
2 teaspoons sweet basil

Leave crabmeat in the shells. Place in a large pot with the oil, onion, parsley and mushrooms. Cook covered over low heat for 30 minutes. Heat all the other ingredients in another pan until they reach the boiling point. Pour sauce over crabs, cover and simmer for an additional 30 minutes. Serve in large soup bowls with garlic bread for dunking. Serves 8.

Crab Chateau

½ lb. crabmeat, flaked
1 small onion, chopped
1 stalk celery, chopped
¼ green pepper, chopped
2 tablespoons butter
½ cup mayonnaise
7 slices bread
butter for bread
2 eggs
¾ cup milk
2 tablespoons dry white wine
⅛ teaspoon salt
dash pepper
½ can cream of mushroom soup

The day before, sauté onions, celery, green pepper in 2 tablespoons butter until golden. Remove from heat and add crab and mayonnaise. Line a shallow pan with 3 slices of buttered bread, cut into 1-inch squares. Put crab mixture on bread and cover with

3 slices of buttered bread, cut into strips. Beat egg and milk together, add wine, salt and pepper and pour over all. Refrigerate overnight. Next day, 1 hour before serving, spread mushroom soup over all and add the 7th slice of buttered bread, cubed. Bake in a 350° oven for 50 minutes. Serves 4. Recipe may be doubled for a party buffet.

Crab Yasas!

½ lb. crab meat
8 tablespoons butter or margarine
½ cup finely chopped onion
¼ cup finely chopped green pepper
½ cup chopped parsley
2 cloves garlic, minced

2 small eggplants
1 cup canned tomatoes, drained
½ teaspoon salt
¼ teaspoon pepper
⅔ cup dry white wine
¾ cup dry bread crumbs
4 strips crisp bacon

Melt butter in a skillet and pour half into a saucepan or small skillet. Sauté onion, green pepper, parsley and garlic in the first skillet until tender. Wash and cut eggplants in half lengthwise and scoop out the pulp. Turn shells upside down in a pan of cold water to prevent discoloration. Chop pulp. Add tomatoes, seasoning, eggplant pulp and wine to the sautéed mixture. Cover and simmer 12 minutes. Add crabmeat. Cook another 2 minutes. Combine the bread crumbs with the remaining butter. Fill eggplant shells with sautéed mixture and top with buttered crumbs. Crumble the bacon and sprinkle over each shell. Pour a little water in the bottom of the baking dish and carefully set the shells in it. Bake in a 400° oven for 30 minutes. Serves 4.

Crab Amontillado

¾ lb. crabmeat
2 packages frozen spinach
6 tablespoons mayonnaise
4 tablespoons ketchup
2 tablespoons chili sauce
4 teaspoons horseradish
2 teaspoons lemon juice
2 tablespoons Amontillado sherry

Cook spinach as directed on the package and drain extra well. Place spinach in a shallow greased casserole. Mix all other ingredients. Spoon crab mixture over spinach. Heat in a 400° oven for 20 minutes. Serves 6.

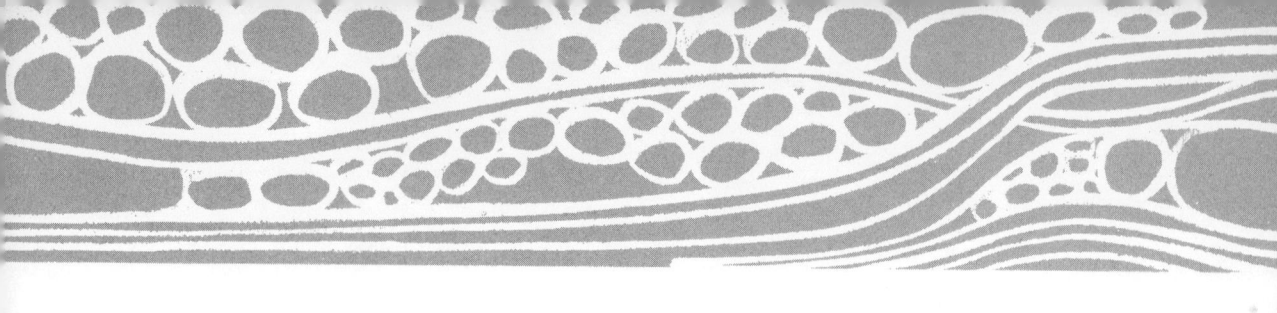

Sea Nip

1 6½-oz. can crabmeat
1 6-oz. package scalloped potatoes
2 tablespoons butter or margarine
1¼ cups hot water
1 tablespoon dry sherry
2 cups half and half or light cream

Empty package of scalloped potatoes into a 1½-quart casserole. Dot with butter. Stir in hot water, sherry, crab and cream. Bake in a 400° oven about 1 hour or until potatoes are tender. Serves 4.

Cockeyed Crab

1 cup crabmeat
8 oz. cream cheese
1 tablespoon mayonnaise
1 teaspoon salt
¼ teaspoon white pepper
¼ teaspoon white pepper
4 shallots, sliced thin
1 tablespoon dry vermouth
2 tablespoons salted peanuts

Beat all the ingredients together (except crabmeat and peanuts) until very smooth. Add crabmeat. Divide into 4 buttered seafood baking shells. Sprinkle with peanuts. Bake 25 minutes in a 350° oven. Serve immediately. Serves 4.

Crab Cuvée

2 lbs. crabmeat
2 cups cooked rice
½ teaspoon salt
dash pepper
2 cans Vichyssoise soup
¾ cup half and half
1 tablespoon dry white wine
½ teaspoon tarragon
½ cup bread crumbs
2 tablespoons butter or margarine

Combine rice, salt, pepper and crab. Mix soup, half and half, wine and tarragon until smooth. Add to crab and rice mixture. Put in a greased casserole. Top with bread crumbs and dot with butter. Bake in a 350° oven for 25 minutes. Serves 6.

John Barleycorn's Crab

1 cup crabmeat
½ cup cooked rice
1 can cream of vegetable soup
2 tablespoons bourbon
2 tablespoons tomato paste

½ teaspoon salt
¼ teaspoon white pepper
red and green pepper for garnish

Butter 3 individual baking dishes. Divide rice evenly in the dishes. Combine all the other ingredients and fill the dishes. Heat in a 375° oven for 15 minutes. Cut red and green peppers into diamond shapes and decorate each dish. Serve immediately. Serves 3.

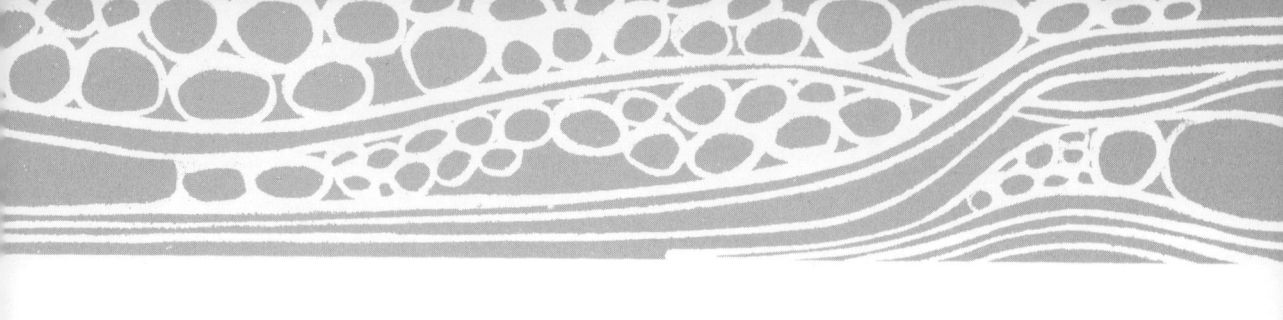

Jugged Crab

1 lb. fresh crabmeat
¼ lb. fresh mushrooms, sliced
4 tablespoons butter or margarine
2 tablespoons flour
½ cup milk
¼ teaspoon salt
dash pepper
½ cup dry white wine
½ teaspoon dry mustard
¼ teaspoon tarragon
¼ cup bread crumbs
2 tablespoons butter

Cut crab into bite-size pieces. Sauté mushrooms in 2 tablespoons butter. Melt rest of butter. Blend in flour and add milk gradually, stirring until smooth. Add wine, mustard, tarragon, salt and pepper and cook for 2-3 minutes. Add crabmeat and mushrooms. Put into an earthenware casserole. Sprinkle with bread crumbs and dot with more butter. Bake in a 350° oven for 30 minutes. Serve with rice. Serves 4 generously.

Light-Headed Crab

½ lb. crabmeat
3 tablespoons butter or margarine
6 eggs
½ teaspoon salt
2 tablespoons sauterne

Heat oven to 350°. On top of the stove slowly melt butter in a 7-inch skillet. Do not allow it to get brown. Beat eggs in an electric mixer at high speed for at least 8 minutes, until bowl is filled with a light foamy mixture. Do not underbeat. Keep beating and add wine and salt. Stop beating and quickly fold in the crab. Pour into the very hot skillet and cook for 3 minutes. Remove from flame and set in oven to bake for an additional 15 minutes. Do not let it get too brown. Cut in wedges. Serve with Mushroom Sauce. Serves 4.

Mushroom Sauce

2 tablespoons butter or margarine
2 tablespoons instant or granular flour
1 cup milk
1 3-oz. can chopped mushrooms, drained
½ teaspoon salt
dash white pepper
¼ teaspoon onion powder
¼ teaspoon paprika

Melt butter and slowly stir in flour. Cook for a minute or two, then slowly stir in milk. Cook until thickened. Add mushrooms and seasoning. Cook another minute. Serve very hot.

Celebration Crab

1 lb. crabmeat
2 tablespoons butter or margarine
1 small onion, finely chopped
½ small green pepper, finely chopped
⅔ cup diced celery
1½ cups half and half
4 oz. bleu cheese, crumbled
2 tablespoons dry sherry
1 cup black olives, sliced
2 tablespoons chopped parsley

Sauté onion, green pepper, and celery in butter until onions are golden. Combine half and half, sherry and bleu cheese in top of double boiler. Heat over hot water (not boiling) until cheese is melted and sauce is smooth. Add sauce, olives and crabmeat to onion mixture. Mix well and heat for about 10 minutes, stirring frequently. Garnish with chopped parsley. Serve with rice. Serves 4.

Crepes Chevalier

1 cup crabmeat
3 tablespoons butter or margarine
1 can cream of shrimp soup
1½ teaspoons instant or granular flour
¼ cup dry sherry
6 crepes

Heat soup and gradually stir in flour. Cook until thick. Sauté crab quickly in butter. Add crab and sherry to soup and stir. Place one crepe at a time in a large, flat oven-to-table dish. Put some crab mixture in one half of crepe and fold over the other half. Repeat until all are filled. Bake in a 325° oven for 10 minutes. Serve immediately. Serves 6 for lunch or 3 for dinner.

Crepes

2 eggs
½ cup water
½ cup milk
½ teaspoon salt
1 cup instant or granular flour
2 tablespoons butter, melted

Combine all ingredients in blender for 1 minute. Brush crepe pan (preferably teflon) with butter. Heat until very hot and pour in a large spoonful of batter. Tilt pan quickly to spread batter. Cook for 1 minute. With a small spatula or your fingers turn the crepe and cook for another few seconds. Repeat until all the batter is used.

Crab Turnovers With Kirsch

½ lb. crabmeat
1 recipe pie crust (or mix) for a double-crust 9-inch pie
1 teaspoon kirsch
1 egg, separated
1 tablespoon minced green pepper
½ can cheddar cheese soup

Set oven at 350°. Roll out crust as thin as possible. Cut into 8 4-inch squares. Beat egg white very stiff. Stir crabmeat, kirsch and green pepper into cheese soup. Fold in egg white. Moisten all the edges of all the squares with a brush dipped in cold water. Divide the crab mixture evenly into the 8 squares. Fold dough over into triangles and seal them firmly. Beat egg yolk and brush the turnovers completely. Bake for 12 minutes. Serve immediately. Serves 4.

Cheers for Crab Quiche

½ lb. crabmeat
1 recipe pie crust (or mix) large enough for a 2-crust pie
6 eggs
1¾ cups half and half
2 tablespoons chablis
1 cup grated Swiss cheese
6 green onions, minced
1 teaspoon salt
dash white pepper

Preheat oven to 350°. Roll out crust very thin and place in a buttered 10-inch quiche pan or pie plate. Place a piece of aluminum foil in the pan on top of the crust and fill with raw beans or rice. Bake for 12 minutes. Remove from oven and discard foil and beans or rice. Beat eggs thoroughly, then add all the other ingredients, combining them well. Pour into crust and bake for 40 minutes or until a knife cut through the custard comes out clean. Serve immediately. Serves 6.

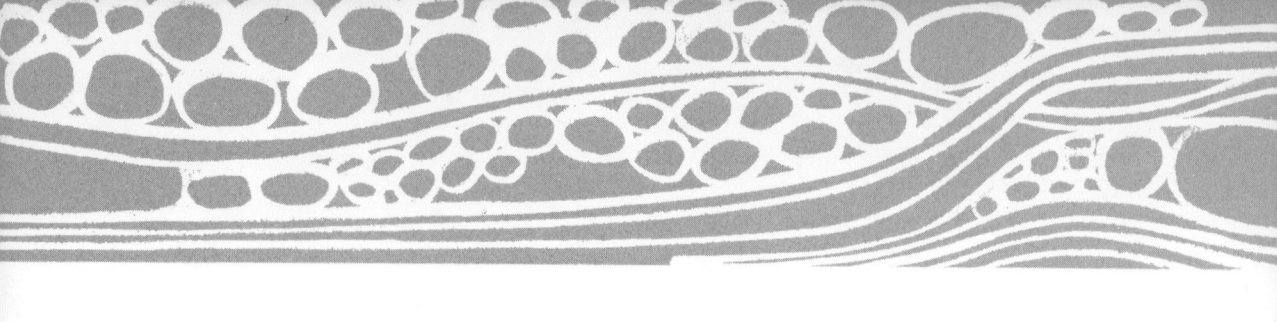

Reveler's Crab Mousse

¾ lb. crabmeat, flaked
1 lb. small fresh mushrooms
3 cups water
½ teaspoon salt
2 tablespoons dry sherry
2 envelopes gelatin
1½ cups sour cream
lettuce or watercress

Clean mushrooms and remove stems. Reserve 12 caps. Chop rest of mushrooms. Simmer gently in 2 cups of water and the salt for 30 minutes. Strain, reserving the liquid. Liquify mushrooms in blender and add to reserved liquid. Cook caps, covered, in 3 tablespoons water for 5 minutes or until tender. Remove caps and add liquid to rest of stock. Add wine. Now measure all the liquid. You should have 2 cups. Add water if necessary. Soften gelatin in 1 cup cold water and dissolve in hot mushroom stock. Refrigerate. When partially set, stir in sour cream and coat the bottom and sides of an oiled 7-cup mold. There should be a half-inch layer at the bottom. Refrigerate mold. When set, dip caps in the gelatin that has thickened but not set and arrange round side down in the mold. Chill mold again for a short time. Fold crabmeat mixture into remaining mushroom mixture and add to mold. Chill until firm. Unmold on lettuce or watercress. Serves 6.

Nectar of the Islands

½ lb. crabmeat
1 bunch romaine, very crisp and cold
1 teaspoon salt
½ pint carton small curd cottage cheese
½ cup mayonnaise
½ cup sour cream
2 oz. Roquefort or bleu cheese, crumbled
1 tablespoon ketchup
1 cup fresh pineapple cubes
1 tablespoon saki
juice of 1 lemon
1 avocado
½ cup grated coconut

Tear the romaine into bite-size pieces and place in a large glass salad bowl. Salt the crabmeat and set aside. Combine all the other ingredients (except avocado, coconut and lemon juice). Add the crabmeat to the dressing. Pour this mixture over the greens. Peel and slice the avocado as neatly as possible into curved thin slices. Place the slices in any desired pattern over the salad. Sprinkle with lemon juice. Toss coconut over the top. Serves 4.

Buy a Crab a Drink!

8 oz. crabmeat
1 bunch watercress
1 large can grapefruit sections, drained
6 tablespoons mayonnaise
3 tablespoons sour cream
1 tablespoon ketchup
1 teaspoon Tabasco
1 teaspoon brandy
1 tablespoon dry sherry
1 teaspoon salt
dash white pepper
paprika
2 lemons, peeled and sliced thin
1 lime, peeled and sliced thin

Line a glass bowl with the watercress. Place the drained grapefruit sections in the bowl. Add crabmeat. Combine all the other ingredients, except lemons, lime and paprika. Stir contents of bowl gently. Dip the lemon and lime slices in a tiny bit of paprika and border the bowl with the slices in an attractive design. Serves 6.

Bacchus's Crab Bisque

1 6½-oz. can crabmeat
1 can pea soup, undiluted
1 can tomato soup undiluted
1 soup can fresh milk
1 teaspoon Worcestershire sauce
2 tablespoons dry sherry

Blend the two soups and heat. Heat milk separately and add to soup gradually with Worcestershire sauce and sherry. Mix and add crab and mix again gently. Heat but do not boil. Serves 6.

Fortified Soupe Mongole

1 6½-oz. can crabmeat
1 can split pea soup, undiluted
1 can tomato soup, undiluted
1 soup can water
2 teaspoons curry powder (to taste)
2 tablespoons dry sherry
salt and pepper to taste

Mix all ingredients and heat. Serves 6.

Crab Apéritif

Crabmeat in bite-size chunks
lemon
soy sauce
dash saki
sesame seeds (optional)

Make a dip of 2 parts lemon to 1 part soy sauce. Add saki. Put bowl of sauce on middle of serving plate. Surround with crab. Garnish with parsley. Provide picks so that guest may spear crab and dip into soy mixture. If you like, you may serve a very small bowl of sesame seeds in which to dip the crab after it has been dipped in the sauce.

CHAPTER EIGHT

ALL TANKED UP

Lobster for a Pink Lady

2 large lobsters, split in half
6 tablespoons butter or margarine
1 teaspoon chicken stock base
½ teaspoon MSG or Accent
2 tablespoons flour
¼ teaspoon salt
⅛ teaspoon pepper
2 cups light cream or milk
1 tablespoon grenadine
1 tablespoon cold milk
½ teaspoon curry powder
4 tablespoons Parmesan cheese, grated
1 small avocado, sliced
1 medium tomato, cut in wedges

Take lobster out of shells and cut into bite-size pieces. Make a cream sauce by melting 2 tablespoons butter. Add the chicken stock base and MSG. Blend in the flour, salt and pepper. Slowly add cream and stir as it heats. Add grenadine. In a separate skillet, heat the lobster in 4 tablespoons melted butter for 3–4 minutes. Mix curry in a tablespoon of cold milk until it is smooth and add to the cream sauce. You may add more curry if you wish, but this should be a delicate flavor. Fold lobster into sauce and put into the shells. Sprinkle with Parmesan cheese. Put under broiler until bubbly and light brown. Garnish with avocado slices and tomato wedges. Serves 4.

Lobster Thermidor, Fino

2 large cooked lobsters, cut in half
3 tablespoons butter or margarine
3 tablespoons flour
1½ cups milk
1 2-oz. can sliced mushrooms
dash paprika
⅛ teaspoon dry mustard
½ teaspoon salt
1 teaspoon chopped parsley or ½ teaspoon dried parsley
¼ cup fino or other dry sherry
3 tablespoons grated Parmesan cheese

Remove meat from lobster shells, carefully. Save shells. Break meat into serving pieces. Melt butter in a saucepan, stir in flour until smooth and add milk gradually, stirring constantly until sauce is thickened. Add lobster, mushrooms, paprika, mustard, salt, parsley and fino to sauce. Spoon into lobster shells. Sprinkle with Parmesan cheese and broil until hot and bubbly. Serves 4.

Cream Sherry, Lobster Newburg

2 cups lobster meat
4 tablespoons butter or margarine
¼ teaspoon salt
¼ teaspoon nutmeg
½ teaspoon paprika
1 cup cream
3 egg yolks, slightly beaten
3 tablespoons cream sherry

Melt butter in the top of a double boiler. Add salt, nutmeg and paprika. Gradually stir in the cream and cook, stirring constantly just to boiling point. Stir a little of the hot sauce into the egg yolks and mix thoroughly. Add yolks to rest of sauce. Cook and stir until slightly thickened. Add lobster which has been broken into bite-size pieces. Continue cooking, stirring over hot water until sauce is thickened (about 10 minutes). Stir in sherry and serve over rice. Serves 6.

Making the Rounds

4 raw lobster tails, sliced in thin rounds
½ cup flour
½ teaspoon garlic salt
4 tablespoons oil
¼ cup dry white wine
½ cup chopped parsley or 3 tablespoons dried parsley
juice of 1 large lemon
1 2-oz. can mushrooms, drained

Remove lobster from shells and slice into fairly thin rounds. Dip in flour seasoned with salt and garlic salt. Fry in oil over high heat for about 2 minutes. Pour off excess oil. Reduce heat and add wine, lemon juice, parsley and mushrooms. Simmer partially covered for 15 minutes. Spoon lobster and sauce over rice. Serves 4.

Lushous Lobster

4 rock lobster tails, cooked and split
¼ lb. fresh mushrooms, sliced
1 medium onion, sliced
4 tablespoons butter or margarine
½ cup dry sherry
1 can cream of celery soup, undiluted
1 teaspoon prepared mustard
dash bitters
dash Tabasco sauce
½ teaspoon dried parsley
dash salt
4 tablespoons Parmesan cheese, grated

Remove lobster meat from the shells, but save the shells. Cut the lobster into bite-size pieces. Sauté the mushrooms and onions in butter until tender. Add wine and simmer for 5 minutes. Stir in soup, mustard, bitters, Tabasco, salt, parsley and lobster. Heat thoroughly. Spoon into shells, and sprinkle lightly with Parmesan cheese. Broil until light brown. Serves 4.

Lobster Wen Lie!

- 1 lb. lobster meat
- 4 tablespoons peanut oil
- 1 tablespoon rice wine
- 2 teaspoons fermented black beans
- 1 teaspoon chopped garlic
- ¼ cup canned water chestnuts, sliced
- 1 teaspoon salt
- ¼ teaspoon sugar
- ⅛ teaspoon pepper
- 2 green onions, chopped
- 1 cup chicken stock
- 1 tablespoon soy sauce
- 2 tablespoons cornstarch
- 3 tablespoons cold water
- 2 eggs, beaten

Pour 2 tablespoons of oil into a 10-inch skillet over high heat. Turn down heat to moderate and add lobster for 1 minute. Stir in wine and remove ingredients from skillet. Add 2 more tablespoons of oil to skillet and add black beans and garlic. Stir. Add water chestnuts and stir. Add sugar, salt, pepper, green onions, lobster and juices. Add chicken stock and soy sauce. Cover pan and bring to a boil. Dissolve cornstarch in water and mix until smooth. Add to pan and stir frequently until sauce is clear. Carefully pour beaten egg into pan in a thin stream. Stir. Serve with rice. Serves 4.

Lobster Caught Red-Handed in the Sauce

1 lb. cooked lobster tails
   sliced in thin rounds
½ cup dry white wine
1¾ cups gruyere cheese,
   shredded
½ cup kirsch
salt
pepper
3 crisp French rolls sliced in
   rounds

Bring the wine almost to a boil in an enamel or earthenware pan. Add cheese slowly and stir with a fork until melted. Add kirsch. Keep stirring and add salt and pepper to taste. Add lobster rounds. The rounds of lobster should be lifted from the fondue with long forks and eaten on a slice of French roll. Serves 3.

Bar Salad

1 cup cooked lobster meat,
   cut in small pieces
1 cup mayonnaise
1 teaspoon Worcestershire
   sauce
½ cup ketchup
1 tablespoon chopped
   parsley
1 hard-boiled egg, chopped
juice of 1 lemon
juice of 1 orange
juice of 1 lime
½ teaspoon brandy
2 teaspoons dry sherry
1 teaspoon Grand Marnier
1 tomato, peeled and diced
romaine lettuce for 4 servings

Arrange romaine on 4 salad plates. In a large crystal bowl place all the ingredients except tomato and lobster. Stir all together. Add tomato and lobster pieces and gently stir again. Serve at the table onto the 4 salad plates. Serves 4.

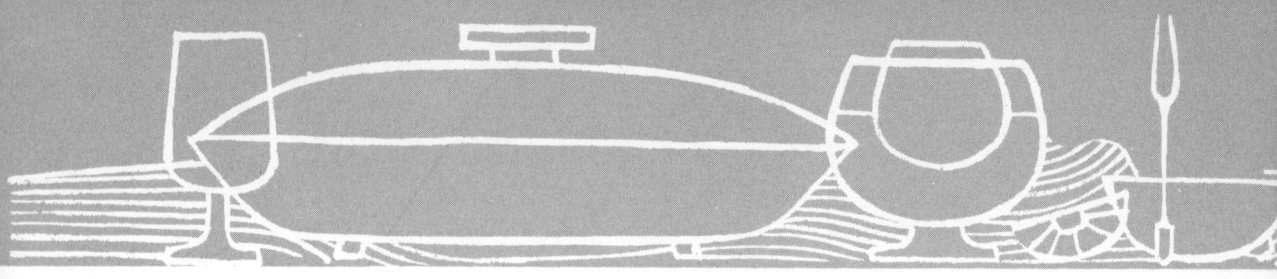

Boiled Clams

4 quarts clams
½ cup water
½ bunch parsley

butter
lemon
dry white wine

Wash and scrub clams thoroughly to remove all sand. Change water several times. Then hold the tail uppermost under running water and all the rest of the sand will be washed out. Place the parsley in the bottom of a large kettle. Add water and clams. Cover tightly and boil until the shells just open (about 6 minutes). Serve in shells in a soup bowl with side dishes of melted butter in which to dip the clams. Add a little lemon and white wine for an extra fillip. Strain the broth left in the kettle and serve in cups or glasses to drink with the clams. Serves 6-8.

Clam Mixers

1 8-oz. can minced clams, drained
12 large mushrooms
½ cup bread crumbs
½ teaspoon onion powder

1 tablespoon dried parsley
4 tablespoons butter or margarine, melted
1 tablespoon lemon juice
1 tablespoon dry white wine

Wash mushrooms and remove stems, leaving a large cavity. Chop stems and add clams, bread crumbs, onion powder, parsley, melted butter, lemon juice and wine. Mix thoroughly. Pile into mushroom cavities and pat lightly to held together. Bake in a 350° oven for 20 minutes. Serves 4.

Chianti Sandwiches

½ cup clams, chopped and drained
1 6- or 8-oz. can marinara sauce
½ cup cooked and flaked leftover fish
¼ cup chianti
8 slices French bread, no thicker than ⅜ inch
3 tablespoons butter or margarine
4 thick slices mozarella cheese
8 tablespoons butter or margarine

Heat marinara sauce. Add clams, fish and wine and heat until steamy. Make 4 sandwiches of the bread, softened butter and cheese. Cut each sandwich in half and fry on both sides in very hot butter. Place 2 half sandwiches on each of 4 plates and pour sauce over them. Serves 4.

Linguini With White Clam Sauce, Frascati

2 8-oz. cans minced clams, including liquor
1 lb. linguini
8 tablespoons butter or margarine
1 generous teaspoon sweet basil
2 large cloves garlic, minced
2 tablespoons dried parsley
1 12-oz. can or bottle clam juice
¼ cup dry white wine
1 heaping tablespoon instant or granular flour
2 tablespoons water
salt
pepper
Parmesan cheese, grated

Cook the linguini in salted boiling water for 7 minutes. Drain well. While the linguini is cooking, melt the butter in a saucepan. Add the garlic, sweet basil and parsley. Mix and simmer for 2 minutes.

Add the clam juice, wine and clams. Mix well and cook slowly until hot. Combine flour and water until smooth. Add to sauce and stir until slightly thickened. Pour sauce into linguini and mix well. Correct seasoning with salt and pepper if necessary and serve immediately. Serve with grated Parmesan cheese. Serves 4.

Hula Loopy

- 1 8-oz. can chopped clams, drained
- 4 green onions, chopped
- 4 water chestnuts, sliced
- 1 cup canned bean sprouts, drained
- 2 tablespoons soy sauce
- ¼ teaspoon powdered ginger
- ½ can cream of celery soup
- ¼ cup grated Parmesan cheese
- ¼ cup dry sherry
- 3 tablespoons shredded coconut
- 1 tablespoon lime juice
- ½ cup chopped macadamia nuts

Combine all the ingredients thoroughly, except macadamia nuts. Put the mixture in a buttered oven-to-table casserole. Bake in a 350° oven for 20 minutes. Remove from oven. Sprinkle with nuts and return to oven for another 5 minutes. Serves 4.

Pie-Eyed Clams

1 8-oz. can minced clams, well drained
1½ cups saltine cracker crumbs
6 tablespoons butter or margarine, melted
2 tablespoons butter or margarine
1 large onion, sliced thin
1½ cups scalded milk (heated just to boiling point)
3 eggs, slightly beaten
1 teaspoon salt
¼ teaspoon pepper
½ lb. cheddar cheese, grated
2 tablespoons dry sherry

Combine cracker crumbs and melted butter. Press the crumbs into a 10-inch pie pan to form a shell. Brown onions until golden in 2 tablespoons butter, and place in bottom of crust. Spread clams over onions. Add scalded milk slowly to eggs, stirring constantly. Add salt, pepper and cheese and stir until cheese is melted. Add sherry. Pour over clams and onions and bake in a 350° oven for 50 minutes. Cool for about 4 minutes before serving. Serves 6.

Chalet Clam Pie

2 8-oz. cans minced clams, including the liquor
1 recipe pie crust (or mix) for 2-crust pie
2 tablespoons butter
2 teaspoons flour
1 egg yolk, beaten
1 teaspoon minced parsley
½ cup half and half
¼ cup dry white wine
¼ teaspoon coarse kosher salt

Line a deep 8- or 9-inch pie plate with pastry. Melt butter and stir in flour. Add the clam liquor. Add all the other ingredients except salt and egg yolk. Cover with an upper crust and brush with egg yolk. Make a few slashes in the crust and sprinkle with coarse salt.

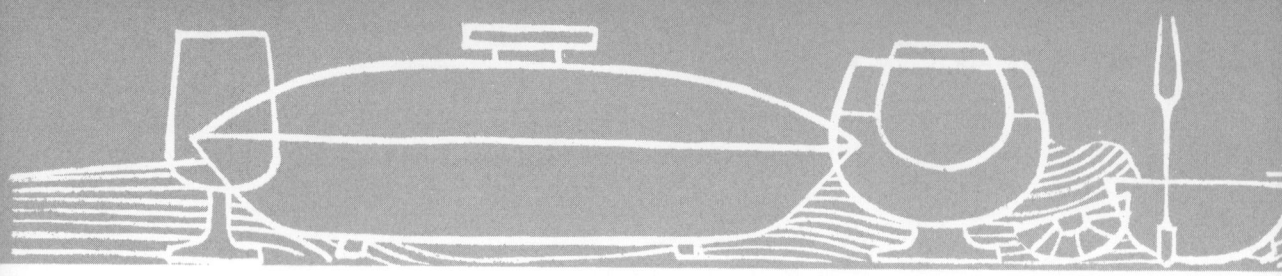

Bake in a 375° oven until crust si brown (about 35 minutes). Serve immediately. Serves 4.

Five o'Clock Fritters

1 8-oz. can chopped clams, drained
1 egg
1 anchovy fillet, minced
½ teaspoon soy sauce
1 teaspoon dry sherry
½ teaspoon salt
¼ teaspoon onion powder
1 cup pancake flour mix to make a fairly stiff batter
peanut oil for frying

Combine all ingredients. Heat oil in small deep pan. Drop ½ teaspoonful batter into oil and fry. Do a few at a time. Keep warm until all are finished. Serve with toothpicks at cocktail time. Makes about 12 fritters.

Cocktail Clams

1 8-oz. can minced clams, drained
½ pint sour cream
¼ small onion, grated
½ tablespoon dry vermouth

Mix all ingredients thoroughly. May be done in advance and refrigerated, but be sure to mix thoroughly before serving. Serve with dip chips.

Oysterman Stewed

16 oysters, fresh or in jars, including liquor
4 cups milk or half and half
½ teaspoon salt
dash white pepper
½ cup dry sherry
4 tablespoons butter or margarine
1 tablespoon Worcestershire sauce
1 tablespoon paprika

Put milk, salt and pepper into a saucepan and scald milk (bring milk to point where the edges are just beginning to boil). Add sherry. In another saucepan melt butter. Add Worcestershire sauce and paprika and turn flame down to simmer. Add oysters. When the edges of the oysters curl, add oysters and juice to the scalded milk and cook gently for 1–2 minutes, depending on the size of the oysters. Serve in bowls with oyster crackers. Serves 4.

To Oysters!

16 small oysters, fresh or in jars
8 oz. fine egg noodles
⅓ cup olive oil
2 shallots, diced
1 cup clam juice
½ teaspoon salt
¼ teaspoon pepper
4 tablespoons dry white wine

Cook noodles according to the directions on the package. Heat oil in a large skillet and cook shallots for 1 minute. Add all the other ingredients, except oysters, and cook for another 2 minutes. Add oysters and cook just until the edges curl. Drain noodles well and divide onto 4 plates. Spoon oysters over the noodles and serve immediately. Serves 4.

All Tanked Up

Spirited Oysters

12 oysters, fresh or
  in jars
6 slices bacon, cut in half
½ teaspoon salt
¼ teaspoon pepper

dash Tabasco
1 teaspoon tomato paste
½ cup Southern Comfort
4 slices toast

Broil bacon until almost done but still limp. Drain well and wrap each oyster in a piece of bacon, tucking the ends under or fastening with a toothpick. Return to broiler and broil for 2 minutes or until bacon is brown. Have prepared 4 small warm plates and 4 slices toast, cut in half. Combine seasoning, tomato paste, Tabasco and Southern Comfort in a small cup over warm water. Place 4 oysters on the toast and pour whiskey sauce over them. Serves 3 as a first course.

Moules Moulin Rouge

2 dozen mussels
1 large onion, chopped
2 cups dry white
  wine

3 tablespoons butter or
  margarine
1 fennel seed

Wash mussels well and scrub them so that all the sand is out. Then wash them again. Put the mussels in a good size pot with the onions, fennel seed, butter and wine. Wine should almost cover mussels; add more if necessary. Cook them over high heat for a few minutes. Cover and cook for about 5 minutes, shaking the pot 2 or 3 times. Serve in large bowls with the onions and liquid poured over the mussels. Serves 3–4.

Stuffed Mussels Bordeaux

12 mussels or clams on the half shell
2 slices fresh white bread
1 tablespoon minced onion
2 tablespoons finely chopped green pepper
2 tablespoons dry red wine
2 tablespoons butter or margarine, melted
salt
pepper

Trim crusts from bread and discard. Make bread crumbs in blender, doing one piece of bread, quartered, at a time. This makes an awful racket, but the crumbs are delicious. Mix crumbs, onion, green pepper, wine, and butter. Salt and pepper may be added to taste. Arrange mussels or clams in shallow baking dish. Cover each with stuffing and bake in a 350° oven for 20 minutes. Serves 4.

Scallops on a Spree

2 lbs. scallops
1 cup French dressing
4 tomatoes, quartered
2 onions, cut in eighths
8 whole mushrooms

Marinate the scallops, tomatoes, onions and mushrooms in the French dressing. If you use a prepared dressing, be sure it's one you're fond of, because the scallops and vegetables take on a little of that flavor. Turn often. Marinate 1 hour at least, 2–3 hours if possible. Put the scallops and vegetables in a shallow baking pan. Pour off most of the marinade, but leave enough so that there is a little left in the bottom of the baking pan. Broil until done. Turn

All Tanked Up

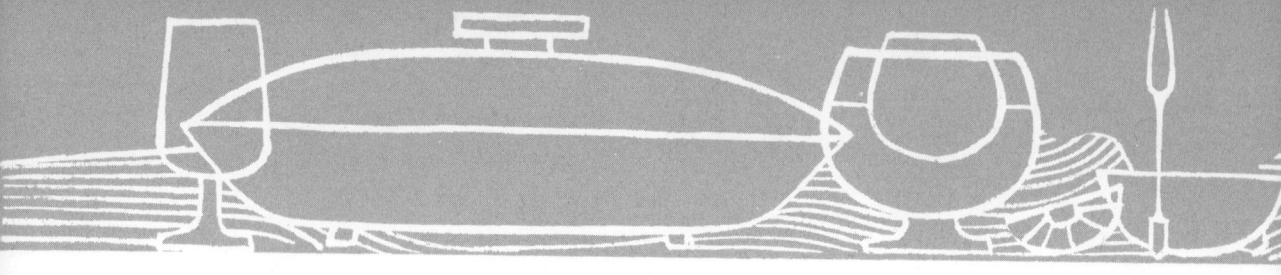

and baste the vegetables and fish often so that they do not cook too fast. Serves 6.

French Dressing

½ cup oil
¼ cup wine vinegar
¼ cup dry white wine
1 scant teaspoon salt
¼ teaspoon pepper
½ teaspoon dry mustard
1 clove garlic, minced

Combine all ingredients well.

Scallops Grappa

16 scallops
1 onion, chopped
4 tablespoons butter
1 clove garlic, minced
1 no. 2 size can Italian tomatoes, drained
¼ cup dry red wine
½ teaspoon salt
8 French-fried onion rings, frozen or canned
1 tablespoon minced parsley

Sauté chopped onion in butter until golden. Push aside, add the scallops and garlic and sauté another 4 minutes. Butter a shallow baking-and-serving dish and place the drained tomatoes in a layer on the bottom. Pour the wine over the tomatoes and then the contents of the skillet. Lightly salt, and sprinkle crushed fried onion rings over all. Scatter parsley over the top. Heat for about 10 minutes or until very hot in a 375° oven. Serves 4.

Happy Hour Scallops

1 lb. scallops
6 slices toasted white bread
½ lb. bacon
½ teaspoon salt
¼ teaspoon pepper

½ cup bread crumbs
4 tablespoons butter or margarine
2 tablespoons dry white wine

Cut toast into 1-inch squares. Cut bacon slices in half and wrap a half slice of bacon around each toast square. Salt and pepper scallops. Alternate scallops and bacon-wrapped toast on small skewers. Place skewers on a foil-lined cookie sheet. Sprinkle bread crumbs over skewers. Heat butter and wine until butter is melted. Put skewers under broiler and baste frequently with the butter and wine until scallops are done and bacon is brown. Serves 3.

Scallops and Sauce

1 lb. scallops
3 tablespoons soy sauce
2 cups sauterne
1 can pineapple chunks, drained

8–12 stuffed olives
1 basket cherry tomatoes
2 tablespoons butter or margarine

Marinate scallops in wine and soy for at least 6 hours. Drain well. Thread on skewers, alternating with the other ingredients. Broil the kabobs on the barbecue grill or in the broiler. Reduce the marinade to about ¾ cup and heat thoroughly. Add the butter. Pass as a sauce for the kabobs. Serves 4.

All Tanked Up

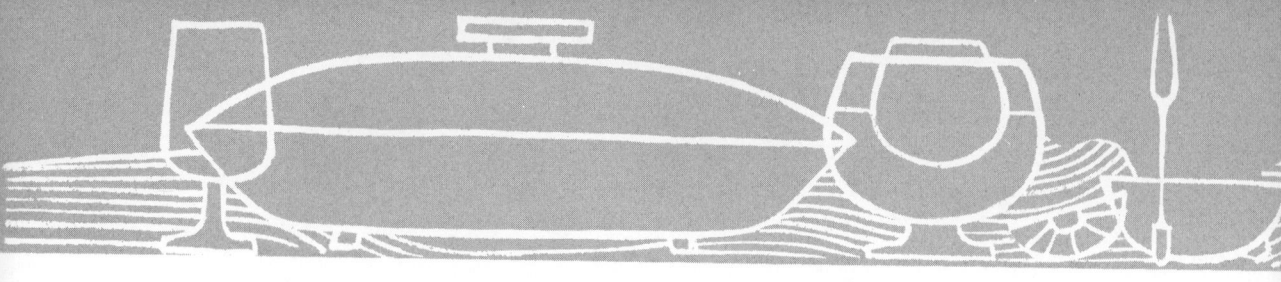

Coquilles St. Jacques, Coup de Blanc

10 oz. scallops, cut in bite-size pieces
½ cup dry white wine
1 shallot, sliced
1½ tablespoons lemon juice
2 tablespoons butter or margarine
¼ teaspoon thyme
¼ teaspoon chervil
3 tablespoons heavy cream
1 egg yolk
2 tablespoons Parmesan cheese

Poach first 5 ingredients 6–8 minutes. Remove scallops and divide into 2 large scallop shells or individual baking dishes. Add thyme, chervil and cream to pan and cook down gently. Add 1 tablespoon sauce to egg yolk, stir well, and add to sauce. Pour sauce over the scallops. Sprinkle lightly with Parmesan cheese. Put under broiler until sauce is brown and bubbly. Makes 2 large portions.

Rumrunner's Scallops

3 lbs. scallops
8 tablespoons butter or margarine
2 cups onions, minced
2 cloves garlic, minced
1 teaspoon salt
2 tablespoons sugar
½ lb. mushrooms, sliced
2 teaspoons curry powder
1 teaspoon fresh grated ginger
2 tablespoons light rum
2 tablespoons cornstarch
4 cups coconut milk
CREAMY NOODLES (See p. 157)
parsley

If fresh or frozen coconut milk is not available, an acceptable substitute can be made by soaking 2 cups dried coconut in 4 cups warm milk. After 15 or 20 minutes, squeeze out the coconut and let the milk cool. Discard coconut. Sauté onions and garlic in 4

tablespoons butter about 10 minutes. Add salt and sugar. Sauté mushrooms in same pan, adding the remaining butter. Cook for a few minutes and add the scallops. Cook slowly 5 more minutes. Add curry and ginger. Taste and correct seasoning. Some additional salt may be desired at this point. Add rum. Sprinkle cornstarch over all, and add cold coconut milk. Cook slowly for 10 minutes. Line a large shallow casserole with creamy noodles and pour scallop mixture over it. Serve immediately, garnished with fresh parsley. Serves 8.

Creamy Noodles

1 lb. package fine egg noodles
8 tablespoons butter
6 tablespoons heavy cream
1½ teaspoons salt

Cook noodles according to directions on package. Drain well and pour into buttered casserole. With a fork quickly stir in butter, cream and salt.

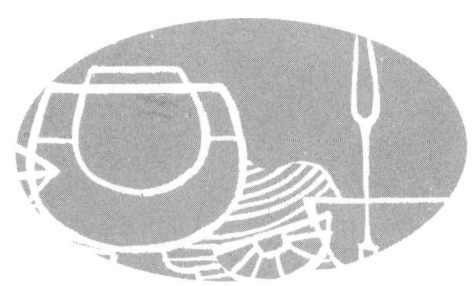

CHAPTER NINE

Sober Sole

2 lbs. fillet of sole
½ cup (approximately) mayonnaise
1 teaspoon salt
½ teaspoon pepper
1 cup crushed corn flakes
2 tablespoons butter or margarine
lemon wedges

Spread both sides of fish with mayonnaise. Sprinkle with salt and pepper. Roll fish in crushed corn flakes and lay in a greased shallow baking dish. Dot with butter. Bake in a 500° oven for 12 minutes. Garnish with lemon wedges. Serves 4.

Finnan Haddie in Moderation

1½ lbs. finnan haddie, cut into 4 pieces
¼ cup milk
¼ cup water
4 tablespoons butter
½ teaspoon (approximately) freshly ground pepper

Put milk and water in a skillet. Add finnan haddie and 1 tablespoon of butter. Cover and bring to a slow boil. Simmer gently for 20 minutes. Drain off the liquid and add the rest of the butter. Sprinkle generously with fresh ground pepper. Cover and heat again for 2 minutes. To serve, remove the fish from the pan and pour the melted butter over the fish. Serve with boiled potatoes. Serves 4.

Reformer's Fish 'n' Chips

2½ lbs. halibut, cod or scallops, or a mixture of all three
1 cup flour
1½ teaspoons baking powder
¼ teaspoon salt
⅛ teaspoon pepper
1 egg
1 scant cup of milk
oil for deep frying
French-fried potatoes or potato chips

Cut the fish into large bite-size pieces. Try to keep the pieces the same size so they'll be done about the same time. For the batter: sift the flour, baking powder, salt and pepper into a large bowl. In a small bowl, beat the egg and add the milk. Mix and stir into the dry ingredients. If the batter seems too thick, add more milk. Pick up each piece of fish with kitchen tongs, dip it into the batter, shake off the excess batter and drop it carefully into hot fat. The temperature should be about 375°. If you don't have a thermometer or a control on your deep fryer, the temperature is right when a cube of bread becomes brown in one minute. Don't overcrowd the deep fryer; fry the fish in batches instead. The fish is done when the crusty coating is golden brown. Serve the fish with either French-fried potatoes or potato chips. Serve with a tartar sauce or a Chinese mustard sauce. Serves 6.

Truite Meunière, Disbarred

4 trout
¼ teaspoon paprika
¼ cup flour
3 tablespoons butter or margarine
2 tablespoons oil
2 teaspoons anchovy paste
juice of ½ lemon
1 tablespoons minced parsley or dried parsley

Dust the fish with flour and paprika. Fry the trout gently in half of the butter and all the oil until brown on both sides. Add more butter if necessary. Remove the trout from the frying pan and keep warm. To pan juices, quickly add anchovy paste, lemon juice, parsley and the rest of the butter. Mix and heat thoroughly. This is done in a matter of seconds. Pour the sauce over the trout, garnish with parsley and lemon, and serve at once. Serves 4.

Perfect Potatoes To Go With Truite Meunière

4 medium-to-large potatoes
¼ teaspoon salt
oil for frying

4 tablespoons butter or margarine
1 tablespoons chopped parsley

Peel and cut potatoes in eighths lengthwise and in thirds crosswise. Parboil in salted boiling water for 5 minutes. Drain thoroughly. Heat ½ inch of oil in frying pan. Add potatoes, shaking frequently and turning when golden brown on one side. Cook until they are done on both sides. Drain off oil and add butter and parsley to the pan. Mix potatoes, butter and parsley. Turn off heat. Potatoes will stay crisp for a few minutes in the pan while you make the sauce for the fish.

Straight Line Trout

4 trout
½ cup or more yellow corn meal
½ teaspoon onion powder
oil
8 tablespoons butter or margarine
4 tablespoons capers, drained
1 lemon, sliced thin

Mix corn meal and onion powder. Roll trout in the mixture until fish is lightly coated. Put oil into a skillet to the depth of ¾ inch. Heat the oil and brown the trout quickly on each side. In a separate pan, melt the butter and add the capers. Put the trout in a shallow pan. Spoon the butter and caper sauce over the fish and broil for 1 minute. Garnish each trout with lemon slices. Serve immediately with remaining butter sauce. Serves 4.

Election Day Perch

8 whole perch
4 tablespoons butter or margarine, melted
½ teaspoon salt
¼ teaspoon paprika
2 cups crushed potato chips

Stir salt and paprika into melted butter. Dip the perch into the butter mixture and then roll in crushed potato chips. Put fish in greased baking pan. Broil on one side only for 6 minutes. Serves 4.

W.C.T.U. Salmon

1 lb. can salmon
4 large onions, chopped
4 tablespoons oil

This is almost like hash, crisp on the bottom and tender and juicy inside. Fry the onions in oil until brown. Add the salmon, including the juices, but remove the center bone. Mix well and turn heat to low. Stir frequently until the juices evaporate. Continue cooking uncovered, at low heat, for about 1 hour or until the bottom becomes brown. Serve immediately. Turn skillet upside down on a platter so that the crust is on top. Scrape the bottom of the pan to get every bit of crust. Serves 4.

Shad Roe Sauté, After Hours

1 shad roe divided in half
4 tablespoons butter or margarine
1 tablespoon shallots or onion, finely chopped
1 tablespoon parsley
pinch sweet basil
½ teaspoon chervil or tarragon
1 tablespoon lemon juice
¼ cup bread crumbs
½ teaspoon salt
¼ teaspoon pepper
1 tablespoon butter or margarine

Sauté the shad roe in 2 tablespoons butter till almost done. This takes only a few minutes on each side. Take the fish out of the pan and keep it warm. In the same pan, add 1 tablespoon butter, shallots, parsley, basil, chervil, lemon juice and bread crumbs. Mix and

brown. Sprinkle with salt and pepper. Now add the rest of the butter. Spread the crumb mixture on the shad roe and serve. Serves 2.

Mrs. Volstead's Hot Crabmeat Puffs

1 8-oz. can crabmeat, flaked
1 cup mayonnaise
¼ teaspoon seasoned salt
2 egg whites, stiffly beaten
4 slices toast
paprika

Mix crab and seasoned salt with mayonnaise. Fold mayonnaise mixture into stiffly beaten egg whites. Pile on toast. Sprinkle with paprika and broil 3 minutes until puffy and lightly browned. Serves 2.

Broiled Lobster A. A. la Roquefort

2 lobsters, split in half
4 tablespoons butter
2 tablespoons Roquefort or
 bleu cheese, crumbled

Dot lobsters with butter and bits of cheese. Broil until lightly brown and bubbly. Serves 4.

Teetotaler's Clam Soufflé

1 8-oz. can minced clams, drained
6 tablespoons butter or margarine
6 tablespoons flour
1½ cups milk (or substitute part with clam liquor)
¼ teaspoon pepper
dash cayenne
6 eggs, room temperature, separated
1 teaspoon salt
2 teaspoons lemon juice
4 tablespoons parsley, chopped fine

Preheat oven to 325°. Melt butter, add flour, blend well and cook over low heat until bubbly but not brown. Add milk gradually. Cook, stirring constantly, until smooth and thickened. Add pepper, cayenne and sauce to egg yolks, beating constantly. Set aside. Add salt to egg whites. Beat until stiff, but not dry. Fold sauce, clams, lemon juice and parsley gently into egg whites. Pour into buttered soufflé pan. Bake for 45 minutes. Don't be impatient and peek. Do not open oven door. Serves 6.

Crumbly Scallops, 1920 Style

1 lb. scallops
1 tablespoon dried parsley
½ cup bread crumbs, more if necessary
1 egg, beaten
½ teaspoon salt
¼ teaspoon pepper
½ teaspoon seasoned salt
2 tablespoons butter or margarine

Wash scallops and dry thoroughly with a paper towel. Mix parsley with bread crumbs. Dip each scallop in bread crumbs, egg and crumbs again. Place scallops in a buttered baking pan. Season with salt, pepper and seasoned salt. Dot each scallop with butter. Broil about 5 minutes on each side. Serves 3–4.

Carrie Nation's Tuna and Spinach Salad

1 7-oz. can tuna, chunk style
1 bunch spinach, cleaned and torn into pieces
6 green or ripe pitted olives, sliced
1 small red Bermuda onion, sliced thin
French dressing

Drain tuna well and break into chunks. Add spinach, olives and onion. Toss with French dressing. Serves 3.

Shrimp Salad
With Curry Dressing for Minors

1 lb. shrimp, cooked and shelled
½ cup mayonnaise
½ cup French dressing
¼ teaspoon curry powder
1 small head lettuce
2 stalks celery, diced
1 green onion, sliced thin
½ teaspoon dill weed

Mix dressing first by combining French dressing and mayonnaise and mixing until smooth. Add curry powder to taste, starting with about ¼ teaspoonful. Add dill weed and mix well. Use 2 or 3 large lettuce leaves as a base on a platter. Shred the rest of the lettuce and put on top of lettuce leaves. Mix shrimp, celery and onion with the dressing and heap on top of the shredded lettuce. Garnish with hard-boiled eggs, tomato and lemon wedges, olives, carrot curls, etc. Serves 3.

Little Astronaut's Salad Ships

1 recipe of SHRIMP SALAD WITH CURRY DRESSING (see p. 168), without lettuce
2 large fresh pineapples
fruit salad made with fruits in season
½ cup sour cream
few drops vanilla

Cut pineapples in half lengthwise (including leaves), and scoop out the fruit. Make a fruit salad with the cut-up pineapple and fresh fruit in season—such as strawberries, oranges, bananas, peaches, etc. Make the dressing for the fruit salad by whipping the sour cream with a fork until light. Add a few drops vanilla and mix well. Add more vanilla if necessary. Put pineapple shells on 4 individual plates. Fill half of each shell with fruit salad and the other half of the shell with shrimp salad. Serve the sour cream dressing separately. Serves 4.

Shrimp in Near Beer

2 lbs. shrimp, shelled
2 cans near beer
½ teaspoon dill weed
½ teaspoon parsley
1 large clove garlic
1 teaspoon salt
½ lemon, sliced

Mix everything but shrimp in a saucepan. Bring to a boil and add shrimp. Reduce heat and simmer gently for about 4 minutes or until shrimp turn pink and are tender. Do not overcook. Drain shrimp and cool. Use as hors d'oeuvres with chili sauce or plain. Serves 6.

Shameless Mary Marinated Halibut or Seviche

2 lbs. fillet of fresh halibut
1 tablespoon salt
⅔ cup lime juice
4 green onions, chopped
½ green pepper, chopped
1 large tomato, peeled and chopped
1 tablespoon chopped parsley
¾ cup French dressing

Cut fish into small, bite-size pieces, mix lightly with salt and lime juice and store in refrigerator 5 hours. Drain well, add the remaining ingredients and marinate 3 hours in refrigerator. Serve with small crackers as an appetizer.

throw salt + lime juice away

86 Cod

4 lbs. ling cod or black cod
2 cups vinegar
4 cups water
1 cup sugar
4 tablespoons pickling spices
1 tablespoon salt
1 teaspoon coarse ground pepper
2 lemons, sliced

Put the vinegar, water, sugar, pickling spices, salt and pepper in a large pot and bring to boil. Taste; it must have a distinct sweet and sour taste. Add more sugar or vinegar if necessary. Cut fish into 2-inch by 4½-inch slices. Roll each piece and skewer together with toothpicks. Taste boiling vinegar and water again before putting fish in, and correct for sweet and sour taste. Lay fish in boiling water gently. Cook at a simmering boil for 20–25 minutes. Cool fish in the liquid about 30 minutes. Put a few lemon slices on the bottom of a crock with a wide neck. Add a row of fish, then

more lemon slices. Alternate fish and lemon, ending with lemon on top. Pour vinegar mixture over all and cover with a tight lid. Cool thoroughly and refrigerate for a week. Serve as an appetizer or first course.

Also speeed w/ a C

Ceviche in a Light Lime Vinaigrette

1# Scallop
1# ahi (tuna)(marlin) 3/4"

Celery
grn. pepper
Red pepper
Red onion
light Vinegarette Dressing
w/ Lime juice
Serve on a bed of shredded cabbage...
Must cook fish then marinate several hours

INDEX

Abbé's Sole 45
Alehouse Shrimp 110
ANCHOVIES
  Toasts 90
Anchovy Mayonnaise 49
Another Round of Bouillabaisse 84
APPETIZERS AND
  FIRST COURSES
    Caviar Sauterne en Gelée 90
    Clam Mixers 146
    Cocktail Clams 150
    Crab Apéritif 137
    Drinker's Cheese 91
    86 Cod 170
    Five O'Clock Fritters 150
    Happy Hour Scallops 155
    Potted Salmon 37
    Shameless Mary, Marinated Halibut or Seviche 170
    Spiked Shrimp Hors d'Oeuvres 121
    Spirited Oysters 152
    Tipsy Tuna 99
    Toasts 90
Apricot Sour Trout 68

Bacchus's Crab Bisque 136
Bar Fly Trout 70
Bar Salad 145
BARRACUDA
  Stuffed Barracuda, Patron 68
Bartender's Halibut 16
BASS
  Bass Bacchanal 23
  Bass Trattoria 25
  Bass With a Head On 22
  Boozy Bass 26
  Cocoloco Bass 27
  Eye-Opener Bass 25
  Fish Cantina 13
  Poisson, Carafe 18
  Taproom Bass 24

  Tippler's Bass 23
  Tutava Tequila 27
  Vintner's Sole 46
  Whiskey Sour Fish 20
Black Cod Bouzo 65
Bloody Mary Shrimp 117
Boiled Clams 146
Bootlegger's Sole 50
BOUILLABAISSE
  Bouillabaisse With Wine #1 82
  Bouillabaisse #2 83
  Bourbon Street Fish Roll 53
  Brandy Snappers 62
  Another Round of Bouillabaisse 84
Brass Rail Perch 79
Broiled Lobster A.A. la Roquefort 166
BUTTERFISH
  Gimlet Fish 78
  Highball Butterfish 79
  Whitefish, Crème Sauterne 76
Buy a Crab a Drink 135

Cakes and Ale 20
Carrie Nation's Tuna and Spinach Salad 168
CASSEROLES
  Alehouse Shrimp 110
  Clubhouse Tuna 98
  Cock-Eyed Crab 128
  Crab Amontillado 127
  Crab Chateau 125
  Crab Cuvée 128
  Here's Tuna 96
  Hula Loopy 148
  John Barleycorn's Crab 129
  Jugged Crab 130
  Schooner Tuna 97
  Sea Nip 128
  Sherried Shrimp and Deviled Eggs 107

Tuna on a Toot 98
Wine Seller's Tuna 96
Wined Shrimp De Jonghe 108
CAVIAR, RED
   Caviar Sauterne en Gelée 90
   Drinker's Cheese 91
   Soupe Superieur 89
Celebration Crab 131
Cellar Pike 67
Chalet Clam Pie 149
Cheers for Crab Quiche 133
Chianti Sandwiches 147
Cioppino 125
Clam Mixers 146
CLAMS
   Boiled Clams 146
   Chalet Clam Pie 149
   Chianti Sandwiches 147
   Clam Mixers 146
   Cocktail Clams 150
   Five O'Clock Fritters 150
   Hula Loopy 148
   Linguini With White Clam Sauce, Frascati 147
   Pie-Eyed Clams 149
   Stuffed Mussels Bordeaux 153
   Teetotaller's Clam Soufflé 167
   Tosspot's Tart 116
Clubhouse Tuna 98
Cock-Eyed Crab 128
Cocoloco Bass 27
COD
   Black Cod Bouzo 65
   Codfish Down the Hatch 64
   86 Cod 170
   Eye-Opener Bass 25
   Fillets, Coup de Vin 64
   Fish and Sweet Potatoes L'Chayim 78
   Fish Cantina 13
   Poisson au Bistro 21
   Reformer's Fish and Chips 162

COLD DISHES
   Bloody Mary Shrimp 117
   Boozy Bass 26
   Connoisseur's Halibut 21
   Mellow Fish 87
   Old Fashioned Fish and Jelly 66
   Reveler's Crab Mousse 134
   Salmon Alaska, Grands Crus 36
   Salmon Cooler 36
   Salmon Out Cold 35
   Shrimp Calvados 116
   Soup on the Rocks 120
   Spiked Shrimp Hors d'Oeuvres 121
   Stoned Cold Salmon with Sauce Verte 34
   Sweet Adeline's Cold Salmon Chaud Froid 34
Cold Yogurt Sauce 79
Connoisseur's Halibut 21
Coquilles St. Jacques, Coup de Blanc 156
CORBINA
   Tippler's Bass 23
Corking Good Red Snapper 63
Court Bouillon 33
CRAB
   Bacchus's Crab Bisque 136
   Buy a Crab a Drink 135
   Celebration Crab 131
   Cheers for Crab Quiche 133
   Cockeyed Crab 128
   Crab Amontillado 127
   Crab Apértif 137
   Crab Chateau 125
   Crab Cuvée 128
   Crab Turnovers with Kirsch 133
   Crab Yasas! 126
   Crepes Chevalier 132
   Double, Sole and Crab 54
   Fortified Soupe Mongole 136
   John Barleycorn's Crab 129

Jugged Crab 130
Light-Headed Crab 130
Mrs. Volstead's Hot Crabmeat
   Puffs 166
Nectar of the Islands 134
Reveler's Crab Mousse 134
Sea Nip 128
Winemaster's Cioppino 125
Cream Sherry, Lobster Newburg 142
Creamy Wine Dressing 120
Crème Sauterne Sauce 77
Crêpes Chevalier 132
Crumbly Scallops, 1920 Style 167
Cucumber Balls, Sautéed 86
Cucumber Sauce 118
Curry Sauce 76

Demon Rum Sole 49
Distiller's Trout 70
Double, Sole and Crab 54
DRESSINGS AND SAUCES
   Anchovy Mayonnaise 49
   Cold Yogurt Sauce 79
   Creamy Wine Dressing 120
   Crème Sauterne Sauce 77
   Cucumber Sauce 118
   Curry Sauce 76
   Eye-Opener Garlic Sauce 26
   French Dressing 154
   Mellow Sauce 87
   Mornay Sauce 45
   Mushroom Sauce 131
   Mustard Sauce 24
   Parsley Sauce 85
   Ripe Olive Sauce 43
   Sauce Verte 34
   Smashed Tuna 99
   White Wine Sauce 22
Drinker's Cheese 91

86 Cod 170

Election Day Perch 164
Eye-Opener Bass 25
Eye-Opener Garlic Sauce 26

Falstaff's Tuna 96
Fillet of Sole with Grapes 44
Fillets, Coup de Vin 64
FINNAN HADDIE
   Finnan Haddie in Moderation 161
FISH, LEFTOVER
   Chianti Sandwiches 147
   High Fish 86
   Smuggler's Fish 85
   Soup Toddy 88
Fish and Sweet Potatoes L'Chayim 78
Fish Cantina 13
Five O'Clock Fritters 150
FLOUNDER
   Flounder Up Tight 56
   Vintner's Sole 46
Fortified Soup Mongole 136
French Dressing 154
Fried Sand Dabs 56

Gimlet Fish 78
Guzzler's Fish 17

HADDOCK
   Poisson au Bistro 21
   Public House Haddock 80
HALIBUT
   Bartender's Halibut 16
   Cakes and Ale 20
   Connoisseur's Halibut 21
   Fish Cantina 13
   Guzzler's Fish 17
   Halibut, Bottoms Up! 19
   Halibut, Bouquet du Vin 15
   Halibut Burgundy 14
   Halibut Kanpai! 15

Halibut Santé 16
Halibut with Rice Wine 18
No Pain Pike 66
Oiled Halibut 17
Poisson au Bistro 21
Poisson, Carafe 18
Rake's Halibut 13
Reformer's Fish and Chips 162
Shameless Mary Marinated
  Halibut or Seviche 170
Whiskey Sour Fish 20
Wino's Sole Amandine 52
Happy Hour Scallops 155
Here's Tuna 96
High Fish 86
High Living Shrimp 119
Highball Butterfish 79
Hula Loopy 148

Innkeeper's Sole 46
Island Binge 75

John Barleycorn's Crab 129
Jugged Crab 130

KIPPERS
  Pub Kippers 88

Light-Headed Crab 130
Linguini with White Clam Sauce,
  Frascati 147
Little Astronaut's Salad Ships 169
Loaded Sole 54
LOBSTER
  Bar Salad 145
  Broiled Lobster, A.A. la
    Roquefort 166
  Cream Sherry, Lobster
    Newburg 142
  Lobster Caught Red-Handed
    in the Sauce 145
  Lobster for a Pink Lady 141

Lobster Thermidor, Fino 142
Lobster Wen Lie! 144
Lushious Lobster 143
Making the Rounds 143

MACKEREL
  Wholly Mackerel 80
MAHIMAHI
  Island Binge 75
  Mahimahi on the Town in Kauai
    75
Making the Rounds 143
MARLIN
  Yachtsman's Marlin 82
Mellow Fish 87
Mellow Sauce 87
Mornay Sauce 45
Morning-After Eggs 88
Moules Moulin Rouge 152
Mrs. Volstead's Hot Crabmeat
  Puffs 166
Mushroom Sauce 131
MUSSELS
  Moules Moulin Rouge 152
  Stuffed Mussels Bordeaux 153
Mustard Sauce 24

Neat Shrimp Newburg 115
Nectar of the Islands 134
Neptune's Harvest 62
Nip of Salmon 29
No Pain Pike 66
Noodles, Creamy 157

Oak Barrel Shrimp 103
Oiled Halibut 17
Old-Fashioned Fish and Jelly 66
Old Soak Shrimp 118
Orange Blossom 81
OYSTERS
  Oysterman Stewed 151
  Spirited Oysters 152

To Oysters! 151

Paella Manzanillo 111
Parsley Sauce 85
PERCH
   Brass Rail Perch 79
   Election Day Perch 164
Perfect Shrimp Subgum 114
Pickled Fish 30
Pie-Eyed Clams 149
PIKE
   Cellar Pike 67
   No Pain Pike 66
   Old Fashioned Fish and Jelly 66
Plastered Salmon 38
Poisson au Bistro 21
Poisson, Carafe 18
POMPANO
   Orange Blossom 81
   Pompano with a Twist 81
Potatoes, Perfect 163
Potted Salmon 37
Pub Kippers 88
Public House Haddock 80

Rake's Halibut 13
RED SNAPPER
   Bass with a Head On 22
   Brandy Snappers 62
   Corking Good Red Snapper 63
   Neptune's Harvest 62
   Snapper Olé 63
   Sweet Sherry Snapper 61
   Whitefish, Crème Sauterne 76
   Winetaster's Snapper 61
Reformer's Fish and Chips 162
Reveler's Crab Mousse 134
Ripe Olive Sauce 43
Rumrunner's Scallops 156

Saki-Eyed Salmon 28

Saki Shrimp, Ami and Kai 114
SALADS
   Bar Salad 145
   Bloody Mary Shrimp 117
   Buy a Crab a Drink 135
   Carrie Nation's Tuna and Spinach Salad 168
   Connoisseur's Halibut 21
   High Living Shrimp 119
   Little Astronaut's Salad Ships 169
   Mellow Fish 87
   Nectar of the Islands 134
   Old Soak Shrimp 118
   Reveler's Crab Mousse 134
   Shrimp Calvados 116
   Shrimp Margarita 119
   Shrimp Salad with Curry Dressing for Minors 168
SALMON
   Bourbon Street Fish Roll 53
   Nip of Salmon 29
   Pickled Fish 30
   Potted Salmon 37
   Plastered Salmon 38
   Saki-Eyed Salmon 28
   Salmon Alaska, Grands Crus 36
   Salmon Cabaret 32
   Salmon Cooler 36
   Salmon from the Winery 32
   Salmon in High Spirits 29
   Salmon in Its Cups 31
   Salmon Out Cold 35
   Sommelier's Poached Salmon Français 33
   Steward's Salmon 38
   Stoned Cold Salmon with Sauce Verte 34
   Sweet Adeline's Cold Salmon Chaud Froid 34
   Vintage California Salmon 30
   W.C.T.U. Salmon 165

Winemaker's Salmon 28
Saloon Shrimp 104
SAND DABS
   Fried Sand Dabs 56
   Tavern Sand Dabs 57
Sauce Verte 34
Sauced Shrimp 115
SAUCES AND DRESSINGS
   Anchovy Mayonnaise 49
   Cold Yogurt Sauce 79
   Creamy Wine Dressing 120
   Crème Sauterne Sauce 77
   Cucumber Sauce 118
   Curry Sauce 76
   Eye-Opener Garlic Sauce 26
   French Dressing 154
   Mellow Sauce 87
   Mornay Sauce 45
   Mushroom Sauce 131
   Mustard Sauce 24
   Parsley Sauce 85
   Ripe Olive Sauce 43
   Sauce Verte 34
   Smashed Tuna 99
   White Wine Sauce 22
Sazerac Shrimp Creole 112
Schooner Tuna 97
SCALLOPS
   Coquilles St. Jacques, Coup de Blanc 156
   Crumbly Scallops, 1920 Style 167
   Happy Hour Scallops 155
   Reformer's Fish and Chips 162
   Rumrunner's Scallops 156
   Scallops and Sauce 155
   Scallops Grappa 154
   Scallops on a Spree 153
Sea Nip 128
Seviche 170
SHAD ROE
   Shad Roe Sauté, After Hours 165
Shameless Mary 170
Sherried Shrimp and Deviled Eggs 107
SHRIMP
   Alehouse Shrimp 110
   Bloody Mary Shrimp 117
   High Living Shrimp 119
   Little Astronaut's Salad Ships 169
   Neat Shrimp Newburg 115
   Oak Barrel Shrimp 103
   Old Soak Shrimp 118
   Paella Manzanillo 111
   Perfect Shrimp Subgum 114
   Saki Shrimp Ami and Kai 114
   Saloon Shrimp 104
   Sauced Shrimp 115
   Sazerac Shrimp Creole 112
   Sherried Shrimp and Deviled Eggs 107
   Shrimp Calvados 116
   Shrimp Cheerio 103
   Shrimp Côté de Provence 105
   Shrimp in Near Beer 169
   Shrimp Margarita 119
   Shrimp Mirin 113
   Shrimp Salad with Curry Dressing for Minors 168
   Shrimp Salut! 112
   Shrimp Sling 106
   Shrimp Swizzle 113
   Shrimp Vino 105
   Singapore Sling Shrimp 106
   Soaked Shrimp 104
   Soup on the Rocks 120
   Soused Shrimp and Asparagus 108
   Spiked Shrimp Hors d'Oeuvres 121
   Tosspot's Tart 116
   Wined Shrimp De Jonghe 108
   Winelover's Jambalaya 109
Smashed Tuna 99

Smuggler's Fish 85
Snapper Olé 63
Soaked Shrimp 104
SOLE
  Abbé's Sole 45
  Bootlegger's Sole 50
  Bourbon Street Fish Roll 53
  Demon Rum Sole 49
  Double, Sole and Crab 54
  Fillet of Sole with Grapes 44
  The Innkeeper's Sole 46
  Loaded Sole 54
  Mellow Fish 87
  Poisson, Carafe 18
  Sober Sole 161
  Sole Cave du Vin 55
  Sole Chablis 50
  Sole Curaçao 48
  Sole Daiquiri 43
  Sole Marsala 47
  Sole on a Bender 51
  Sole on Tap 48
  Sole Saturnalia 44
  Sole Vin du Pays 53
  Vintner's Sole 46
  Whiskey Sour Fish 20
  Wino's Sole Amandine 52
Sommelier's Poached Salmon
  Française 33
SOUPS
  Bacchus's Crab Bisque 136
  Fortified Soupe Mongole 136
  Oysterman Stewed 151
  Soup on the Rocks 120
  Soup Toddy 88
  Soupe Superieur 89
Soused Shrimp and Asparagus 108
Spiked Shrimp Hors d'Oeuvres 121
Spirited Oysters 152
Steward's Salmon 38
Stoned Cold Salmon with
  Sauce Verte 34

Straight Line Trout 164
Stuffed Barracuda, Patron 68
Stuffed Mussels Bordeaux 153
STURGEON, SMOKED
  Morning-After Eggs 88
Sweet Adeline's Cold Salmon
  Chaud Froid 34
Sweet Sherry Snapper 61

Taproom Bass 24
Tavern Sand Dabs 57
Teetotaler's Clam Soufflé 167
Tippler's Bass 23
Tipsy Tuna 99
To Oysters! 151
Toasts 90
Tosspot's Tart 116
TROUT
  Apricot Sour Trout 68
  Bar Fly Trout 70
  Distiller's Trout 70
  Straight Line Trout 164
  Trout With a Bun On 69
  Truite aux Boites 71
  Truite Meunière, Disbarred 162
TUNA
  Carrie's Nation's Tuna and
    Spinach Salad 168
  Clubhouse Tuna 98
  Falstaff's Tuna 96
  Here's Tuna 96
  Schooner Tuna 97
  Smashed Tuna 99
  Tipsy Tuna 99
  Tuna on a Toot 98
  Tuna Ties One On 95
  Wine Seller's Tuna 96
TUTAVA
  Tutava Tequila 27

Vintage California Salmon 30
Vintner's Sole 46

W.C.T.U. Salmon 165
Whiskey Sour Fish 20
White Wine Sauce 22
WHITEFISH
  Fish and Sweet Potatoes
    L'Chayim 78
    Whitefish, Creme Sauterne 76
    Whitefish Prosit! 77
WHITEFISH, SMOKED
  Morning-After Eggs 88
Wholly Mackerel 80
Wine Seller's Tuna 96
Wined Shrimp de Jonghe 108
Winelover's Jambalaya 109
Winemaker's Salmon 28
Winemaster's Cioppino 125
Winetaster's Snapper 61
Wino's Sole Amandine 52

Yachtman's Marlin 82

NOTES